ALEX KARADZIN

Joe Rogan: How to Win The Game of Life

Success, Habits, Mindset and Life Lessons

Contents

Introduction   iv

1   Joe Rogan Origin Story   1

2   Modern-Day Renaissance Man   8

3   Raw Authenticity   22

4   World-Class Discipline & Work Ethic   42

5   Charisma   62

6   Final Words   80

Gift For You   85

About the Author   88

Also by Alex Karadzin   91

Introduction

Joe Rogan is one of the most influential people of today.

While his status is unquestionable, his path to success has been particularly interesting and captivating. From a martial artist, actor and comedian, UFC commentator and analyst, to hosting the most popular podcast in the history of the internet.

His journey to the top is incredible, but the road Joe took was an unconventional path to massive success.

What is fascinating about Joe is the fact that he had one of the most diverse careers any major influencers ever had. As you'll read later on in this book, everything Joe did in life was simply following his north star. A man of strong convictions, Joe isn't willing to compromise on his integrity and values.

Evident by his unusual life journey and body of work, Joe has always done things his way.

Somehow, Joe was always a pioneer and a trailblazer. A little-known fact about him is that he was one of the first celebrity bloggers on the internet. According to a Wayback machine and the internet archive, Joe had a fully functional blog in August of 2000.

Joe decided to jeopardize his rising career in the most powerful industry in the world, to explore this new 'thing' called the Ultimate Fighting Championship. At the height of his popularity, and with a promise of making it big in

Hollywood, Joe Rogan went to Dothan, Alabama to be a backstage and post-fight interviewer.

Laughed at, criticized, and misunderstood by most, Joe couldn't care less about the external noise. He just loved fighting and was passionate about being a part of the history in the making.

For 25 years, Joe is the face and voice of the biggest MMA promotion in the world. He became a household name within the ever-growing fighting community and fans.

Some would argue that he had a sixth sense about trends in the future. However, there is no argument that Joe Rogan never followed trends, he was creating them. In 2009 when streamed his first live show, many internet and content experts believed that long-form conversations will never find their audience.

Eleven years later, Joe Rogan is the undisputed king of all podcasts and a trendsetter who showed us what is possible. His show, the *Joe Rogan Experience* is one of the most valuable shows in the world, at around 100 million dollars.

My initial goal with this book was to find a way to model Joe Rogan's approach to life and to create an applicable framework for success.

To do that, I wanted to answer the question:

How do you win at the game of life?

Later on, as I delved deeper into the research of Joe Rogan's unique personality and the manner in which he goes through life, seemingly out of nowhere, a new question arose:

Is it really about winning at the game of life or....

How do you play the game?

Without a shadow of a doubt, Joe Rogan is the winner. He was successful at almost everything that interested him, including martial arts, stand-up comedy, and having long-form conversations for the world to hear.

However...Joe Rogan never chased success and material wealth. Somehow, success always found him.

Joe Rogan: How to Win in The Game of Life is my hardest attempt to encapsulate Joe's wisdom and offer a blueprint anyone could apply in their own life. Just like in all the other books from the *''Success Leaves Clues''* series, I broke down the mindset, attitude, behavior, habits, life perspective, and lessons for success.

Before we dig deeper into Joe Rogan's authenticity, personality and charisma, we have to cover the foundation by looking at life circumstances and events that shaped him.

No better place to start than at the Joe Rogan origin story.

1

Joe Rogan Origin Story

"Be the hero of your own story." - Joe Rogan

Joe Rogan was born in Newark, New Jersey, on August 11th, 1967. His formative years were turbulent, as his earliest memories are of his father abusing his mother. When Joe was five, his mother divorced her husband and later remarried when Joe was seven. They have also moved to San Francisco and according to Joe, he had a happy childhood aside from the fact that he was constantly alone.

Both his mother and stepfather were hard-working people and even when they were at home, they would just watch tv, as they were tired from work. Because of that, Joe had a lot of freedom from a very young age, and he would often wander the streets and explore the city of San Francisco.

The family later moved to Gainesville, Florida, and then to Boston where Joe would enroll in Newton South High School.

While attending high school, Joe Rogan made a decision that would change the course of his life forever.

During a lunch break, Joe got into a fight with another kid who threw him to the ground and decided not to punch him. It turned out that the other kid was a wrestler and he knew how to fight. For Joe, the feeling of being helpless and left to the mercy of another was a feeling he never wanted to experience again in his life.

Although the event was traumatic and humiliating, it was also one of the life-changing experiences that Joe would forever be grateful for. Soon after, Joe started practicing karate and a year later, he enrolled in taekwondo classes.

For the first time in his life, Joe found his purpose. Moreover, this was the first time that he didn't feel like an insecure loser. He fell in love with martial arts and he was obsessed with his training and dedication to the sport. After a while, Joe started competing at various tournaments and he was starting to get recognized at the state level.

At the age of 19, Joe Rogan won the US Open Championship taekwondo tournament as a lightweight. He was a Massachusetts full-contact state champion for four consecutive years and became a Taekwondo instructor.

When he was 20, Joe decided to try boxing and kickboxing. As soon as he did, he realized that he had a distorted perception of his fighting abilities. Other boxers and kickboxers would regularly beat Joe in sparing sessions. Disillusioned with taekwondo, Joe transitioned to kickboxing.

After amassing an amateur record of 2−1 in the kickboxing ring, Joe was convinced that his calling was to become a professional. However, around this time, he started experiencing massive and frequent headaches and he feared he might sustain worse injuries.

In what he described as a serendipity moment, Joe decided to try his luck with another passion—Stand up comedy.

Before his fights, Joe was nervous, and to alleviate the stress and tension he would tell jokes and make his teammates and fellow fighters laugh. Seeing that Joe had a talent for making people laugh, his friends encouraged him to try stand-up comedy.

After six months of preparation, he performed his first stand-up routine on August 27, 1988, at an open-mic night at 'Stitches' comedy club in Boston. To this day, Joe remembers this night clearly and vividly.

He remembers how terrified he was before stepping up to the stage. Joe said he was so terrible and that he bombed hard. (To bomb as a comedian means that your jokes don't go over with the crowd and get no laughs. Typically, when a comic says they "bombed," they are referring to an entire set.)

Despite his lackluster debut, Joe fell in love with the craft. He loved the adrenaline rush he felt when he was on stage, which is something he previously only felt when fighting. Unlike fighting, the biggest damage you could sustain in comedy was bruised ego if you underperform.

Around this time, he knew he had to make a choice between fighting professionally and stand-up comedy. For Joe, the decision was quite easy and he decided to hang up his gloves and retire from kickboxing.

For the next six years, Joe would work diligently on his stand-up craft, getting better and better. During this time, he had to work numerous jobs to support himself financially. Those jobs included: teaching martial arts at Boston University, delivering newspapers, driving a limousine, doing construction work, and completing duties for a private investigator.

In 1990, Joe Rogan moved to New York City to pursue his dreams of being a full-time comedian. However, his big break happened in 1994 when he moved to

LA. Soon after arriving in the city of angels, he performed on the MTV comedy show *Half-Hour Comedy Hour.* This appearance led to wider exposure and soon after, he started receiving acting offers.

In the same year, Joe landed his first acting role in the sitcom *Hardball,* where he played a role of a young, brash, and self-centric baseball star. Although the show was canceled after eight episodes, Joe would soon find a new acting gig. From 1995 to 1999 he starred in a sitcom *NewsRadio,* as an electrician and handyman Joe Garrelli.

Looking back at this role, Joe believes it was a dream job as it granted him financial security while he was working on his stand-up as often as he could.

In 1997, Joe had another life-shifting moment, when his agent told him about a potential gig and he was absolutely certain that Joe would pass on the opportunity. A new fighting organization called *'Ultimate Fighting Championship* was in dire need of an interviewer for the events, and Joe jumped on the opportunity. At the time, UFC was an unsanctioned sport and was labeled as *'human cock-fighting'* by the media.

Years later, Joe remembers how the movie industry and especially producers of the *NewsRadio* told him that his association with this new and emerging sport would jeopardize his acting career.

Joe couldn't care less, as he felt deep down that this 'new thing' will be huge and he wanted to be a part of its inception. Besides, Joe Rogan was a genuine martial artist and the UFC seemed like the ultimate martial art, as it combined various standing, grappling and ground fighting aspects. The name of this new sport was mixed martial arts (MMA), and the UFC organization was the pioneer in the industry.

UFC became a global phenomenon over the next 25 years, and the company is worth around 4 billion dollars (2021). Joe Rogan became synonymous with the brand as he holds a position of an analyst and commentator for almost every fighting event the company produces. Needless to say that Joe made the right decision when he decided to align himself with the UFC and mixed martial arts sport.

At the turn of the century, Joe was on a roll as in 1999 he recorded his first comedy special '*I'm Gonna Be Dead Some Day...*' which was released in August 2000. The special received national exposure and after 12 years of hard work and dedication, Joe was acknowledged as one of the hottest commodities in the world of stand-up comedy.

In 2001, another intriguing offer came Joe's way, a tv show called '*Fear Factor*'. Joe was approached to host the show, and although he was initially skeptical, in a typical Joe Rogan way, he decided to go with the flow.

The reason for Joe's hesitancy was the premise of the show. Contestants were required to complete three jaw-dropping stunts in exchange for $50,000. Those who failed or backed out were eliminated from the competition. These stunts included consuming live spiders, sheep eyeballs, and maggots in pursuit of the prize. The only reason why Joe accepted the offer to host the show was to observe anecdotes and stories and use them for his stand-up comedy.

Much to Joe's surprise, the show lasted from 2001–2006 as it ran for 6 seasons and 144 episodes in total. During this time Joe got more than enough stories for his comedy acts, and solid financial stability from a hefty paycheck that allowed him to focus exclusively on his stand-up.

For the next few years, Joe worked hard and diligently on his comedy career. Being a host of '*Fear Factor*' helped him a lot, as the show increased Rogan's national exposure which caused turnouts at his stand-up gigs to grow. He recorded and produced a few more specials and established himself as one of the most popular and successful comedians.

In 2009, Joe made a decision that will forever change his life and elevate his status to superstardom. The decision was made out of necessity, as Joe

Rogan moved back to California with his family, which was a decision he reluctantly made. According to Joe himself, he was frustrated and was looking for something to occupy his mind. That something was a weekly broadcast show in the form of a podcast.

On the 24th of December 2009, the first episode aired and it had around 200 people who were watching it live. They had no idea that they were witnessing history in the making.

As usual, Joe was persistent and dedicated and by August 2010, the podcast was formally named *The Joe Rogan Experience*, in an homage to The Jimi Hendrix Experience, and aired live several times a week. Joe was fortunate to be the early adopter of the new emerging format of content delivery which was the podcast form.

However, his meteoric rise and success on the internet have to be attributed to his insane work ethic and consistency. (We will explore his work ethic and discipline in a later chapter)

The 2010s were a highly successful decade for Joe.

Aside from his podcast that became his full-time job, Joe was involved with multiple other projects. He was still heavily involved with the UFC, and by the end of 2020, Joe Rogan is one of the most decorated MMA analysts. He won numerous MMA awards and he is one of the most recognizable faces of the UFC multimillion-dollar brand.

By the same token, Joe established himself as one of the most successful comedians in the 2010s. He released six comedy specials to a pretty much positive response from both the critics and fans. His last two specials: '*Triggered*' (2016) and '*Strange Times*' (2018) were picked up by Netflix which allowed him to reach an even wider audience. Although, by this point in his career, Joe Rogan became a household name in the world of stand-up comedy, mixed martial arts, and one of the biggest internet influencers of all time.

By the end of 2020, *Joe Rogan Experience* has become one of the most downloaded podcasts in the history of the internet. His youtube channel alone that contains a video format of the recorded podcasts, has more than a billion total views. His guest list includes world-renowned intellectuals and philosophers, scientists, A-list celebrities, and other notable guests from all walks of life.

In September of 2020, Joe Rogan signed an unprecedented exclusive deal with Spotify worth around 100 million dollars. This deal represents the pinnacle of Joe Rogan's career as it symbolizes the value Joe brings to the world and his immense influence on the cultural landscape. In other words, in terms of reach and exposure, Joe has become one of the most powerful people on the planet.

In the following chapters, we are going to deconstruct Joe's model of success by breaking down his intricate patterns of behavior, unique life perspectives, and action models that made Joe a winner in the game of life.

2

Modern-Day Renaissance Man

"There's a very famous Miyamoto Musashi quote.

Once you understand the way broadly, you can see it in all things.

The idea is once you understand what excellence is all about, whether it's in painting, or carpentry or martial arts, that you see how that excellence manifests itself in any discipline.

I think that all the different things that I do enhance all the other things that I do." – Joe Rogan

In today's day and age, we are taught that in order to be successful — we have to choose a specific path.

We are encouraged by the social norms to find our passion as soon as possible and stick with it until that passion translates into a massive success. Unfortunately, success is not a linear path, a simple black and white spectrum. More often than not, it's gray and the road to success is uncertain.

The best representation of this philosophy of commitment to a singular goal is the famous *10 thousand hours rule.*

In case you are not familiar with it, the rule states that in order to master a craft, you need to invest 10 thousand hours of deliberate practice. The author of this rule, Malcolm Gladwell, argues that mastering any skill, from playing the violin to becoming a chess master requires diligent practice, time, and effort.

Since 2008 when his book 'Outliers' came out where he proposed this idea, many of his contemporaries, scientist and researchers criticized his proposal stating that Gladwell oversimplified historical, cultural, and complex social phenomena in order to prove a point about mastery.

Truth be told, there are countless examples that confirm Gladwell's notion of mastery and success.

One of the most famous examples has to Tiger Woods.

Tiger Woods is probably the best golfer in the history of the sport. Ever since he was a baby, his path seemed already predetermined. When he was 2 years old, he was already a golf prodigy, appearing on national television and making headlines in the most prominent newspaper of that time.

Tigers father, Earl Woods, recognized talent in his son and for the next few years, he coached and trained him. If there was ever any doubt about the trajectory of Tiger's life and career, they were squashed by the age of 8. The young prodigy already won all the major championships he could, often competing with older boys and regularly winning.

By the age of 20, Tiger Woods was already a pro, signing the most lucrative deal in the history of golf, with Nike. Aside from playing and practicing, Tiger had little time and interest for other things boys of his age might have. His talent was obvious from an early age, but what made him a master was years of honing and polishing that talent.

In other words, Tiger Woods is a specialist and he was one from a very early age.

Another, equally adequate example of massive success through specialization and dedication to one thing exclusively, are the Williams sisters. Venus and Serena Williams were both former №1 ranked tennis players, they have won all the major tournaments and championships in this sport.

Richard Williams, Serena's and Venus's father, decided that his daughters will be world-class tennis players, even before they were born. At the age of four and a half, two sisters took the tennis racket, and under the watchful eye of their father and coach, started their career and life journey.

By the age of 14, both sisters have turned pro and the rest is history.

Just like Tiger Woods, growing up, both of Wiliams sisters had very little time for anything else than tennis. According to Richard himself, after watching Virginia Ruzici play, he decided that his daughters will be professional tennis players. He even went as far as creating a 78-page manual for training, as well as taking both sisters to public tennis courts before they were five years old.

While Richard Williams's obsession with the idea of raising two tennis champions and robbing them of childhood can be questioned, the matter of fact is that the names of Venus and Serena Williams will forever be etched in the history of the sport. Their legacy and accomplishments will stand long after both of them are gone.

The examples of Tiger Woods and Williams sisters clearly show that dedication to a singular goal and persistence can undoubtedly lead to massive success. While the road to success can be a linear path to follow, evident by the examples above, more often than not that road is curved and skewed with many diverging paths showing up as we walk.

Although those paths are diverging, eventually, they all lead to the same destination – to the top of the mountain.

Unlike Tiger Woods or the Williams sisters who were lucky enough to discover their talents from a very early age, most of us will inevitably struggle to do the same well into our 20s, 30s, or even 40s. Unfortunately, some will never discover those inner talents or find what makes them tick—what makes them feel alive.

* * *

"The only reason why I went back to school was that I didn't want to be a loser. All of my friends were in college, and I was the only one who didn't. I didn't want to go to college, I just didn't know what was my next step in life. After half of the semester, I received a call from the dean telling me that I have to write a letter and explain my absence from school.

Basically, they told me I have to present a compelling case as to why they shouldn't expel me.
So I did.

I wrote this bullshit letter where I said how difficult my life was at the moment but how I want to remain at the university despite the difficulties. I worked so hard on that letter and I was just lying and bullshitting them.

I was also bullshitting myself. I didn't want to go back to school. I thought to myself, If I put half of the effort into my studies, tests and exams as I have in this letter, I would easily graduate.
That's when I realize, I didn't want to do it.

I didn't see the point in college and I just couldn't force myself anymore. I was scared and I had no direction in life. I was pretty stressed out about my future, I just couldn't see myself working regular 9–5 jobs. Luckily, this was when I became serious and committed to my stand-up career.
"

For someone who has a 30-years long illustrious career, Joe ended up in the stand-up comedy world by chance rather than by choice. He certainly chose to be an entertainer and do comedy but it was a set of unusual circumstances that led him to make that career choice.

It was a group of his closest friends who gave him a nudge in the right direction and at just the right time. In his early martial arts career, Joe often used to ease the tension with humor before matches and during the competition.

Joe loved comedy from an early age. However, it was *Richard Pryor: Live on the Sunset Strip* that touched him on a profound level. According to Joe, nothing ever made him laugh like the movie, and especially Richard Pryor's comedy act.

Joe's love for humor and comedy was certainly deeply ingrained in him.

His massive success and longevity were anything but certain, though. Through every step of the way, Joe had to navigate obstacles and hurdles. Even hardcore gamblers wouldn't bet on Joe to make it as far as he did.

In fact, many were predicting Joe's career to take a deep dive after his unexpected success in Hollywood.

His level of success and fame reached a national level fairly quickly and quite unexpectedly. (Which is a pattern that shows up in Joe's life every once in a while)

After securing a spot on MTV's *Half Hour Comedy Club,* Joe passed his biggest challenge yet and passed it with flying colors. He nailed the performance and the audience loved every second of his act. The network's executives were blown away and wanted to sign an exclusive contract. Joe had other plans, and he decided to wait for other offers to come in.

And they did, in bunches.

After negotiating with interested networks, Joe decided to sign a development deal with Disney. They have recognized Joe's talent and a desire to succeed and awarded him an opportunity to make a television debut. By 1995, he was cast as Frank Valente, a young and eccentric baseball player, in a new FOX sitcom called *Hardball.*

The show didn't make it past the 8th mark episode but Joe's career was on an upward trajectory.

A new NBC show was on the horizon and Joe was about to hit a lucky break, just six months after arriving in Hollywood. In a moment of serendipity, NBC executives and the producers of *NewsRadio* decided to make a last-minute change just before the production started. Actor and comedian Ray Romano was replaced because his style of comedy didn't gel with the rest of the cast.

Joe Rogan was brought in as the last replacement and he was the final piece that was missing to make the show a standout on the network.

The last-minute switch caused Joe to work closely with the writers of the show in order to flash out and polish his character. By this point, Joe was already writing his stand-up material but working with professionals helped him elevate his writing skills to an entirely new level.

Unexpectedly, Joe found himself in the heart of Hollywood, in one of the most powerful industries in the world.

He was surrounded by the best of the best the industry has to offer. Joe got a unique chance to learn from the most gifted writers, and creative geniuses while being a part of the *NewsRadio* tv show.

Pretty early on, Joe understood how the television and movie industry works and realize that his career path is not the one on either small or big screen. The last time Joe had such an important life decision to make was when he flunked college and stumbled upon a new path of stand-up comedy.

In 1999, things were different for Joe. He wasn't lost and directionless anymore.

Now, Joe was certain about pursuing mastery in his comedy craft while at the same time being open to other interesting projects that will light a spark and excite him. Looking at the choices Joe Rogan made throughout his life, excitement needs to be a prevailing element for any of Joe's endeavors.

At the turn of the century, Joe was on a roll and he was heavily involved with multiple projects. He opted to sign an exclusive three-album deal with *Warner Bros. Records* and he began tentative plans to star in his own sitcom on FOX, called the *Joe Rogan Show.*

According to Joe himself, he was excited and passionate about his show and the preproduction development was well underway when something else turned up on the horizon.

In a typical Joe Rogan fashion, he scrapped those plans and accepted an unusual offer.

In 2001, a new NBC show was the talk of the town and the entire Hollywood. The premise was quite simple: Contestants go through a series of extreme and bizarre challenges and stunts in order to win a prize of $50,000. The only thing that was missing from the equation was the host. The only reason why Joe accepted the invitation was so that he can observe and collect material for his stand-up comedy. He was convinced that the show would not last, simply because of its preposterous premise.

Little did Joe knew at the time, but the show ended up being one of the most popular shows on the network, with an original run lasting for five long years. Moreover, the show was syndicated and started airing on other networks including FOX, UPN, WB network and cable channel FX.

Joe's popularity skyrocketed around this time, which was evident by the drastic increase in turnouts on his comedy shows. Joe continued to host the *"Fear Factor"* but his heart wasn't in it. Years later, Joe admitted that after a while, he was hosting the show simply to get a lofty paycheck.

A blessing in disguise came in 2006 when the show was canceled after record-low ratings.

With a hefty sum he earned from the show, Joe hired two people to film him and his comedy friends on tour and he posted those clips on his website that was fully functional from the early 2000s.

Another element of Joe's curious nature translated into a blogging and vlogging venture. In fact, back in the day, Joe was a pioneer in the blogging field. According to the Wayback Machine and the internet archive, Joe had a fully functional blog in August of 2000.

In 2000, not many people were convinced that this new thing called the internet would eventually revolutionize the world. Joe relied on his experience from Hollywood and the vast knowledge he picked up in the writers' room and effectively translated it onto his blog. On top of all of his accomplishments and ventures, even his faithful audience forgets that Joe is a prolific writer.

He has been a writer since the beginning of his stand-up career in 1988. He became consistent and picked up steam once his blog was up and running and he just kept the momentum going to this very day.

In 1994, the year after the UFC's inception, Joe witnessed a fighting tournament event that would forever change his life. (The frequency and the intensity
of these life-changing events are a recurring theme in Joe's life)

A Brazilian named Royce Gracie won the tournament, after beating four guys
in one night. (In succession, not all at once, of course)

What was particularly and even more fascinating about Royce was that he
was significantly smaller than all of his opponents. He was also a master of
martial arts that was unknown to the US, and the rest of the world, at the
time—**Brazilian Jiu-Jitsu (BJJ)**

That night, Joe's entire paradigm about fighting and mixed martial arts
changed. He realized that a new martial art that can revolutionize the fighting
landscape is on the horizon. Joe being the explorer that he is decided to
immerse himself into the sport of BJJ.

Once again, like so many times before and after, Joe was an early adopter.
Nowadays, BJJ is a legitimate sport and a self-defense discipline taught in
martial arts schools all over the world.

However, in the late 90s, many professional fighters didn't know about the BJJ,
let alone fighting commentators and hosts. Joe's first term with the UFC lasted
for around two years, after which he quit. Although Joe loved the fighting
business and his gig, it was simply unsustainable for him to keep going.
    Fighting events were often held in rural places, and Joe had to cover all of
the expenses himself. Moreover, Joe's stand-up career and his acting were
suffering as a result.

His Jiu-Jitsu training helped him make a transition to the UFC and color
commenting. Joe's knowledge of the ground aspect of professional mixed
martial arts fights served him perfectly. Because of his popularity and
semi-celebrity status back in 1997, but more because of his actual skills and

knowledge he brought to the mix, the UFC management wanted to make him a part of the company.

There were other b-list celebrities they could've approached for the job, but none of them had what Joe had — The experience and passion for fighting and martial arts. By this time in the late 90s, Joe was already a practitioner of a new martial art form, besides taekwondo and kickboxing.

In 2001, after the UFC was acquired by the new management.

The new president, Dana White had big plans for the organization. Unlike the previous owner, Dana wanted to shape the UFC into a legitimate sport. The road ahead of him and his team was long and uncertain, but Dana knew what was the very first step on that road.

Dana approached Joe with an intention of rehiring him and giving him a new position in the company. This time around, instead of being a backstage interviewer, Joe would be commentator, calling the fights in the octagon. Dana's move was quite simple: Leverage on his increasing popularity, his love for the sport, and his deep knowledge of the martial arts.

Luckily for them, the second time they came to offer him the commentary position, Joe had a simple request. Joe didn't want any money. He wanted free tickets for fighting events, for him and his friends.

After about a few months and fifteen free gigs as a commentator, Joe accepted a full-time paid job. Nearly 20 years later, he still holds the same position. In the meantime, Joe Rogan won multiple prestigious MMA awards, including Wrestling Observer Newsletter Award for Best Television Announcer twice, and was named MMA Personality of the Year four times by the World MMA Awards. More than his awards, his legacy is forever etched and intertwined with the sport of MMA.

From humble live stream beginnings to the most influential podcast on the internet

On the 24th of December 2009, Joe Rogan ventured into uncharted territory, once again. Out of necessity as much as out of his curiosity, Joe and his friend Brian Redban recorded their first live stream. On that live stream, the two men talked about various topics while around 200 people were watching.

Little did they all know at the time, but that night, they were witnessing history in the making.

As much as Joe was excited about his new project, the sheer excitement alone wasn't the only reason he started regular live streaming. Joe and his family moved back to LA, from Boulder, Colorado. Undoubtedly, the move was in the Rogan family's best interest but for Joe personally, coming back to Los Angeles was coming back to the hell he already barely escaped, or so he thought.

He needed a new distraction to occupy his mind and for him to channel all the intensity in something he never tried before.

After the first couple of episodes, Joe started inviting other people to the live stream, including his friends from the stand-up comedy world. Ari Shafir, Joey Diaz, and Duncan Trussel were among the first guests. What was particularly interesting was the format of the show.

Many of the JRE episodes are well over two hours long. Back in the early 2010s, such a long-form conversation was inconceivable as many so-called internet marketing and psychology experts claimed people want to be able to hold the attention on the audio for that long. Joe Rogan lead by example and showed that attention span is not an issue. Boring content and a presentation are.

JRE is unique, and as much as some are trying to copy the formula, the ingredients Joe brings to the table are uniquely his. Joe's guests over the years included some of the most brilliant minds this planet has ever seen.

By the end of 2020, *Joe Rogan Experience* has become one of the most downloaded podcasts in the history of the internet. His guest list includes world-renowned intellectuals and philosophers, scientists, A-list celebrities, and other notable guests from all walks of life.

Joe Rogan is also a master conversationalist who always gets the most out of his podcast guests. (We'll touch more on his unique charisma later in this book)

While comedy is a highly subjective matter and what someone deems funny, others may not. However, after 30 years in the business, Joe Rogan has certainly achieved mastery over the matter. Moreover, his life-long martial arts experience made him a legendary commentator in the field of Mixed Martial Arts.

* * *

"Jack of all trades, master of none"

You've probably heard this expression before. Essentially, it describes a person who dabbles in many activities and ventures but never sticks around to become good at it. More importantly, the expression is used in derogatory terms to discredit the individual in question.

The original expression was actually used as a compliment.

"Jack of all trades"

roughout the years, the extension *''master of none''* was added to
.

Did you know that one of the most famous and influential figures in Western art history, Vincent Van Gogh, had several careers, each of which he deemed a true calling?

One of the greatest minds in the history of humankind, Albert Einstein regularly played the violin while taking a break from many of the complex equations he was constantly solving throughout his career.

Benjamin Franklin, one of the founding fathers of the United States, was also a highly accomplished writer, scientist, inventor, statesman, diplomat, printer, publisher, and political philosopher.

The above-mentioned polymaths are just a small portion of those who made history and shaped the world we live in. They were outliers who dared to be different and left their legacies as true mavericks.

These people who left the mark were not just generalists. No, they were specialized generalists. A unique bread of individuals who pursued and often achieved greatness in many different disciplines and crafts.

While being committed to a singular goal, and a linear path can and will lead to prosperity in life, it's not the only way to succeed.

In today's day and age, our value as individuals is often measured through the monetary perspective. For that reason, the sense of exploration is heavily discouraged by society, and instead, we are encouraged to choose a profession as soon as possible and stick with it. Hopefully, a profession that pays well.

We live in a world where instant results are a measure of overall success. Having this short-term mindset in an ever-changing world can have detrimental consequences on our well-being.

We want what comes the fastest, but often and usually what's best for us is what comes in the long run. Joe Rogan is a perfect example that shows us the importance of playing the long game.

What's fascinating about Joe Rogan isn't the transition between one venture to another, but the manner how he switched between those ventures. Also, the way he used his experience, knowledge and skills from previous endeavors to create a completely new path.

Joe Rogan is a renaissance man who is an evident example that generalists can become masters in their respective fields. He defied the '10 *thousand rule specialist'* wildly adopted by society as the only norm of mastery and massive success.

More than that, he showed us by example that creating your own path rather than following someone else's footsteps can lead to incredible rewards in life.

Joe Rogan is the epitome of the expression:

''Jack of all trades. Master of some''

In the following chapters, we'll explore his unique personality and how he became a specialized generalist. The one that influences and shapes the world in front of our eyes.

We'll focus on answering the following question:

''*How did Joe Rogan become a master of his craft?*''

3

Raw Authenticity

"My act is so completely and totally uncensored that the only way I could really pull it off is if I treat the audience like they're my best friends." – Joe Rogan

"Hey man, I got a show you something..."

My friend had this concerned look on his face, and at first, I thought something serious happened to him. Little did I know — to him, it was quite a serious matter he wanted to show me.

I felt nervous and anxious, as he was the guy who always had a big smile on his face. My high school friend was always ready to crack a joke and make everyone around laugh wholeheartedly. From the moment I met him, he told me that his dream was to be a professional stand-up comedian.

As a matter of fact, he was the guy who introduced me to the wonderful world of stand-up comedy. Every Friday night, after school, I would come to his house and we would watch comedy shows long into the night.

This Friday night was supposed to be no different. But it was.

As I was entering his living room, he had his laptop opened and connected to the TV screen. The screen was static and paused, as he was obviously waiting for me to play the clip from Youtube.

Confused and taken aback by this unusual reception, I looked at the screen and saw his favorite comedian:

Carlos Mencia.

He pressed the play button and right from the getgo it was clear that Carlos was arguing with some guy big guy in a jacket, who wore his hat backward.

> *''What's going on here?''*

> *''Man, Carlos is a thief. He stole jokes and bits from so many comedians. I just spent a few hours investigating, and it's all true.''*
> *''Alright. What's up with the security guy?''*
> *''That's not a security guy. That's* Joe Rogan. *He is also a comedian and, apparently, he is the only one who stood up to Carlos''*

This was the first time I'd seen my joyful friend so utterly devastated. This was the first time I heard the name, *Joe Rogan.*

Back in the early 2000s, one of the most popular and powerful comedians on the scene was Carlos Mencia. At the height of his fame, Carlos had an HBO special, his show on Comedy Central and he won numerous comedy awards.

There was just one problem.

Carlos Mencia was a thief.

He would blatantly steal jokes from his fellow comedians, famous and non-famous alike. Although he was a thief, no one dared to stand up to him because Carlos was very influential and had powerful friends in the industry. For less known comedians, speaking up against Carlos Mencia would mean the end of their career as comedy clubs always took the side of a golden goose who brought profit and exposure.

It was an open secret in the industry but no one spoke up against Carlos.

This incident wasn't the first nor the last time, Joe Rogan went against the grain and did things his way. Joe stayed true to himself despite the repercussions he knew he would inevitably face. Because he filmed the heated argument, the comedy store banned Joe for two years. Moreover, his agency fired him as a client because the same agency was managing Carlos Mencia.

For any other comedian, being blacklisted from the industry would be a fatal career blow, but not for Joe Rogan. Joe wasn't just a comedian and the incident helped him get exposure, as his popularity started to rise from that moment. More importantly, Joe Rogan earned the respect of his fellow comedians for standing up to Carlos Mencia, a guy who was notoriously disliked by his peers in the comedy scene.

This incident became known as the "Carlos Mencia incident" and would forever change the nature of stand-up comedy and the landscape of the scene. As a result, Carlos Mencia's career was effectively over that night as he was branded as a joke thief. After this incident, comedians were less likely to steal jokes or rip off fellow comedians, as they were well aware of the consequences.

Speaking of consequences, Joe was well aware of what will happen to him if he stood up to the mighty Carlos Mencia. He knew he will be ostracized from the stand-up industry and that his livelihood will be in jeopardy. As mentioned, that is exactly what has happened to Joe. Although he had support from fellow comedians, that support means a little when no one wants to hire you or work with you.

By directly confronting and recording an incident with Carlos Mencia, Joe Rogan was willing to put his career on the line, if needed to put an end to Carlos's blatant intellectual property theft.

Joe was emotionally involved as Carlos has stolen from Joe's friend, Ari Shafir.

If there is something one should never do if decides to provoke or cause Joe to react in a vicious manner - It's messing with his friends and family. This was a fatal mistake a poor Carlos made. He stole too many times, and he stole from Joe's friends.

In spite of the danger of being blacklisted from the industry, Joe willingly took the risk while putting a final nail that was Carlos Mencia's career. For Rogan, this action was non-negotiable.

Why did Joe Rogan put his career on the line to stand up to Carlos Mencia and protect his friend?

Because Joe Rogan is a man who values friendship and comradery. One of his core values is relationships and loyalty.

Joe has a large circle of people, but his closest friends have been there for decades. Not only that his friendships are long but they are also intense, which only solidified those bonds. For anyone looking to understand what Joe Rogan is about, there is a video on youtube where Joe talks about his friendships and expresses his gratitude.

Joe Rogan is the man who realized that success is worthless if you have no one to share it with. Because of his outlook on life and personal philosophy, his friends love to be around him. He is often ruthless in his honesty, even if the truth is not something a friend would like to hear. Ultimately, Joe knows that by holding back from speaking up, he is effectively doing his friends a disservice, or even worse – putting them in danger.

This was the case with Joe's friend Brendon Schaub.

Brandon is a former MMA fighter and a former heavyweight in the UFC. In fact, in the UFC organization, the two started hanging out and spending time together. Joe Rogan took young Brandon under his wing and took over the role of mentor.

However, not before Joe crushed a brutal truth blow to his loving friend in a live podcast. Joe Rogan had to intervene to save his friend, on a talk that took place on Dec 11, 2014.

> Joe Rogan: *"A lot of things looked bad about the fight.... You looked very stiff. You didn't look fluid.... You didn't look like you were well prepared... . Your movement just didn't look like an elite fighter's movement.*
>
> *I worry about your commitment to fighting, and I worry about where you stand."*
>
> Brandon Schaub: *"Really? I disagree."*
>
> Joe Rogan: *"The reality of your skillset, where you're at now. I don't see you beating the elite guys. If you had a wrestling match with Cain Velasquez, how well do you think you'd do?*
>
> Brandon Schaub: *"I think people would be surprised."*
>
> Joe Rogan: *"I think you'd be surprised. I really do. I think he'd f—k you up.... There's a bridge between you and the best guys in the world. And I*

don't know if you can cross that bridge. That's the reality of life.

I worry more about you than I do about them…. What I'm saying, I say with love. A hundred percent. I'm not saying this to hurt your feelings. That's the last thing I want to do. If I didn't love you, I wouldn't be willing to do this. And I wouldn't want to do this."

Although Joe regretted his decision to intervene in a live program with a live audience in attendance, Brandon had the right to know the truth. No one from Schaub's social circle had the guts to be the messenger of misery, which is exactly what Joe knew he had to do. His friends deserve Joe to be the voice of reason when needed. Otherwise, Brandon could end up with a serious injury or lifelong damages.

Instead, Brandon took a new direction in life.

Six months after the night of the harsh truth, Brandon is successfully building his career as a stand-up comedian. In 2019, Brandon filmed his first comedy special, fittingly named – *You'd be surprised.*

Joe spent most of his life in regular introspection as he tried to understand himself and the world around him. His love and support for recreational drugs are well known and documented.

His appreciation of weed is only paralleled by his appreciation of life itself.

Joe's appreciation for the mystery of life is best reflected in his other core value - Freedom.

As a seven-year-old, Joe would roam the streets of San Francisco while his mom and stepfather were at work. By his account, this was the first time he felt freedom as he was exploring the unknown territory having moved from Boston and an oppressive and controlling father.

Although an idea of a seven-year-old kid roaming the streets of a city might sound dangerous, Joe felt liberated in his adventure. The practice of exploration in his formative years played a huge role in Joe Rogan's perspective and the manner in which he moved through life. In 2009, Joe moved back to LA and came close to slipping into a serious depression and unhappiness.

He often speaks about his impression of Los Angeles, and it's evident that to him, ironically the city of angels is a hell hole. Unsurprisingly so, considering that Joe moved from nature-oriented Boulder, Colorado. In 2020, the Rogan family moved to a beautiful mansion in Lake Austin, Texas.

Looking back, we can safely conclude that Joe made his decisions in life by aligning the potential experience of his choice with his core values. This is especially true for major life decisions he had to make, most notably a decision about his career.

By his own admission, he was clueless as to what his professional path would be.

As a teenager during summer break, Joe would find work in different industries. His summer jobs included being a cook, a dishwasher and an assistant to a private investigator. Before he started teaching taekwondo and earning a living as an instructor, Joe worked as a construction worker. His stepfather was an architect who set him up with construction work.

While working on a construction, 16- year old Joe Rogan, learned the importance of hard work and manual labor. More importantly, young Joe realized what he doesn't want to do in life.

Although Joe speaks fondly of his time spent working on a construction, he admits this experience made him question his future. For the first time, Joe Rogan knew he needed a plan as he didn't want to work as a construction worker for the rest of his life. By the same token, Joe was honest to himself about a regular 9-5 job and the life it entails.

Deep down, Joe knew what was important to him in life and in his career. He wanted *freedom* in every sense of the world. Joe values the *freedom* to move and explore, and the *freedom* to express himself.
    All of these criteria were checked as Joe was determined to become a martial artist, but as he grew older so did the doubt in his fighting abilities.

Ultimately, the fear of being seriously hurt, damaged and the fear of lasting damages prevailed as Joe gave up on his dream of becoming a professional fighter. Instead, he found a new calling in life. More accurately, Joe stumbled upon a new path that changed his life trajectory forever. Joe Rogan discovered stand-up comedy, a craft that satisfied the same yearning for freedom as fighting. (Minus the potential brain damage)

Joe Rogan's yearning for freedom is perfectly manifested and exemplified in his adventurous spirit and curiosity mindset.

It was because of the curiosity mindset that he tried his hands in the stand-up. Growing up, Joe didn't see himself as particularly funny but his friends thought otherwise. As a youngster, he was a fan of comedy but never in a million years could he imagine that one day his name would be mentioned in the same breath with comedy legends and his role models including Richard

Jeni, Lenny Bruce, Sam Kinison and Bill Hicks.

Joe Rogan's curiosity is clearly evident from the fact that he became the most successful podcaster on the internet. Not only that Joe is the most successful and influential, but he is also a pioneer who paved the way for podcast format. Before Joe Rogan came to the scene, long-form conversations were not nearly as popular as today.

Having a conversation with anyone for three hours could be exhausting, but listening to Joe Rogan having a conversation with his guests can make three hours pass in a heartbeat.

Joe's curiosity is reflected in the way he is conversing and asking well-thought and meaningful questions. That curiosity led to vast knowledge on various topics and issues which is why Joe Rogan can hold his own even when talking with the most brilliant minds on the planet. Joe draws references from his broad spectrum of interests, passions and life experience and makes any conversation intriguing, interesting, and seldom memorable.

Furthermore, Joe is a humble guy who has his ego in check.

He is willing to learn from those who know more than him. Each one of his 700 guests taught gave Joe and his audience a nugget of wisdom, a memorable personal story, a mindblowing idea, or just sparked a curiosity in listeners to learn more about a particular subject.

On the road to success, Joe has met a lot of people from all walks of life. The more successful he got the more toes he stepped on in the process. However, even those who dislike Joe or aren't fans of his work, can't deny one thing about him:

Joe Rogan is real.

In the sea of noise, his voice and message to the world stand out. Joe attracts people because he is authentic. He knows who he is and his actions are aligned with his core values and beliefs.

Through regular introspection, Joe discovered and is in process of discovering and acting upon his true self.

He is confident in who he is and how he comes across. Joe is not afraid to speak up his mind on issues he feels strongly about, even if it goes against popular opinion. He is always willing to question the status quo because he knows that deep down he is an explorer.

Joe Rogan's authenticity is firmly anchored in his values and beliefs. He is a man who values *freedom and exploration, friendships and family, discipline and mastery.*

* * *

How to Discover Your Values:

Before we dig deeper into the 'how to' part, let's first address the "why" aspect of the equation. Knowing who you are entail having a sense of self which means having an established value system you rely on to guide you through life.

If you haven't clearly defined your values, you can end up making choices that conflict with them. When your external actions conflict with your internal value system, the result is usually frustration, unhappiness, and an inevitable serious depression down the line.

Maybe you have a vague idea about the things you care deeply about or maybe you haven't had a chance to sit down and check-in with yourself so far. Maybe your circumstances didn't allow you to do so or the timing for unraveling wasn't right, but whatever the case may be, keep in mind that having values and more importantly acting in accordance with them will keep you from simply drifting along in whichever way life is pulling you.

Furthermore, having and knowing your values will give you the courage and confidence to make the right choices based on those values. Whenever faced with a dilemma, you can turn inwards and ask yourself the following:

"Is this action aligned with my values, with who I am and who I strive to be?"

"If yes, how so? If not, why not?"

Your answer will illuminate the decision.

Two crucial elements of finding your values

I will have to keep you waiting just a little longer as we address crucial elements of discovering your values: *Environment and Process.*

Knowing how to approach such a complex notion of discovering your values is half of the battle won. Establishing an environment and process will help you get in the right state of body, mind, and spirit.

Before you start, make sure you have the proper environment in place. Having a nice and quiet place for this exercise is paramount to your success. We live in a fast-paced, hectic world with daily responsibilities and to-do lists where the only measure of success is how productive we were and how many things we managed to accomplish by the end of the day.

For this reason, I strongly advise doing this exercise during the weekend or your day off from work. You need to be at 100% of your capacity if you want to get the most out of the experience. To do that, you have to remove the noise around you or remove yourself from the noise.

Emails, notifications, the internet, as well as other people, are a distraction you should eliminate before you start. For this reason, the first step is to ensure you have a nice and quiet place where you will be relaxed and comfortable.

Many of my students and friends who did the same exercise told me that the best place to do this self-assessment activity is outdoors. The possibilities are endless, you could take a walk in a park, sit on a bench by the water, or meditate and relax in nature.

The second step is to get a designated journal.

Journaling is one of the most underrated and underappreciated skills you could develop in your lifetime. It's one of the activities that yield the best results, a hack to exponential growth. If you already have one, use it. If not, I wholeheartedly recommend getting one.

Alternatively, you could use paper. However, what comes out of you and onto this piece of paper will be extremely valuable and you should make sure you keep it close to you at all times. I strongly advise against using the computer or writing software for this activity. Mostly, because of the aforementioned reasons of distraction.

Ideally, you want to keep technology use at a minimum. Also, using pen and paper to jot down your thoughts allows your mind to wander and which is exactly the state of mind and spirit you want to be in. It's been scientifically proven that writing and journaling the old-fashioned way with a pen and paper drastically improves your creativity.

The third step is to ask yourself a deep probing question.

What is truly important to me?

Allow your mind to go as far back in the past as possible and think about the moments that made you feel alive or when you've been the happiest. Don't rush the process to get to the outcome. Write down whatever comes to mind that you feel is useful for you and be honest with yourself. Remember, no one else is going to see this journal. Don't censor yourself or edit as you write.

Once you feel ready, it's time to actually note down your values.

For your convenience, I've put down a list of the most common values that you can use as a reference. Go down the list and write 5 values in your journal you feel the most connected to. If you think you have more than five, that's fine. Write them down anyways, and once you are finished listing down the values, you will prioritize them in the next step and remove them until there are five values on your list.

- Acceptance
  - Accomplishment
  - Accountability
  - Accuracy
  - Achievement
  - Adaptability
  - Adventure
  - Alertness
  - Altruism
  - Ambition
  - Awareness
  - Balance
  - Beauty
  - Boldness
  - Bravery

- Brilliance
- Calm
- Candor
- Capable
- Careful
- Certainty
- Challenge
- Charity
- Cleanliness
- Clear
- Comfort
- Commitment
- Communication
- Community
- Compassion
- Competence
- Concentration
- Confidence
- Connection
- Consciousness
- Consistency
- Contribution
- Control
- Conviction
- Cooperation
- Courage
- Creativity
- Credibility
- Curiosity
- Decisiveness
- Dedication
- Dependability
- Determination

- Development
- Devotion
- Dignity
- Discipline
- Discovery
- Drive
- Effectiveness
- Efficiency
- Empathy
- Empower
- Energy
- Enjoyment
- Enthusiasm
- Equality
- Excellence
- Experience
- Exploration
- Expressive
- Fairness
- Family
- Fearless
- Ferocious
- Fidelity
- Focus
- Foresight
- Freedom
- Friendship
- Fun
- Generosity
- Genius
- Giving
- Grace
- Gratitude

- Greatness
- Growth
- Happiness
- Hard work
- Harmony
- Health
- Honesty
- Honor
- Hope
- Humility
- Humor
- Imagination
- Independence
- Individuality
- Innovation
- Inquisitive
- Insightful
- Inspiring
- Integrity
- Intelligence
- Intensity
- Intuitive
- Joy
- Justice
- Kindness
- Knowledge
- Leadership
- Learning
- Liberty
- Logic
- Love
- Loyalty
- Mastery

- Meaning
- Moderation
- Motivation
- Optimism
- Order
- Organization
- Originality
- Passion
- Patience
- Peace
- Performance
- Persistence
- Playfulness
- Potential
- Power
- Productivity
- Professionalism
- Prosperity
- Purpose
- Quality
- Reason
- Recognition
- Recreation
- Reflective
- Respect
- Responsibility
- Results-oriented
- Reverence
- Rigor
- Risk
- Satisfaction
- Security
- Self-reliance

- Selfless
- Sensitivity
- Serenity
- Service
- Sharing
- Significance
- Silence
- Simplicity
- Sincerity
- Skillfulness
- Solitude
- Spirit
- Spirituality
- Stability
- Status
- Stewardship
- Strength
- Structure
- Success
- Support
- Surprise
- Sustainability
- Talent
- Teamwork
- Temperance
- Thankful
- Thorough
- Thoughtful
- Timeliness
- Tolerance
- Toughness
- Traditional
- Transparency

- Trust
- Truth
- Understanding
- Uniqueness
- Unity
- Valor
- Victory
- Vision
- Vitality
- Wealth
- Winning
- Wisdom
- Wonder

In case you have more than five values on your list, see if you can combine them into one. If you have two complementary values, for example: "exploration" and "adventure", feel free to combine them into one *"exploration and adventure"*.

If you did the above step right, your list should look something like this:

- Freedom
- Exploration and Adventure
- Joy
- Connection and Relationships
- Growth

Now, it's time to make your values action-oriented.

Joy — Radiating Joy

Growth — Seeking Growth

Freedom – Being Free

Connection and Relationships – Experiencing genuine human connection and relationships

Finally, let's make them uniquely yours.

Take your action-oriented values and make your personal statement. This personal statement is a code of conduct that will serve as a north star on your life journey. The internal compass that you can always rely on, no matter what.

Radiating Joy

I am a bringer of light. I shine my light on everyone around me. No matter how hard I work, or how much I suffer, I always find a way to stop and smell the roses because life goes by too fast.

Seeking Growth

My being is composed of three aspects: Physical, Mental, Spiritual. I am actively seeking growth in each one and all three combined. Every day in every way, I am growing, getting better and getting stronger.

Being Free

I am a being created with free will. I get to design my life and create my experience by choice and not by chance.

Congratulations!

You have just discovered your values. More importantly, you have put them on paper and in a framework. In case you are stuck and can't complete the exercise - that is perfectly normal, especially if this is the first time you are doing this value extraction activity. This is not an exercise you should force in any shape or form. Let it come to you and whenever you feel ready, jump right back into it and complete the exercise.

4

World-Class Discipline & Work Ethic

"Joe's found success in absolutely everything he's done. His work ethic is otherworldly." — Joey Diaz

One of the universal truths of life says: Action speaks louder than words. To get a real sense of a person, pay close attention to what they do rather than what they say. Joe Rogan can talk the talk, but it's easy to see that he walks the walk.

When it comes to his insane discipline and work ethic, Joe Rogan leads by example.

Working in the personal development industry, I have witnessed one of the biggest challenges people have, which is the lack of productivity.

Whether it's the artist, the entrepreneur, fitness enthusiast, the struggle is real. Some are desperately trying to be consistent at what they do, some are unable to establish routines that will lead to the desired outcome, while others just want to be more efficient with their endeavors.

In other words, they just want to get s*it done.

As a master procrastinator myself, I can understand and relate to the struggle. On top of that, I am the ultimate day-dreamer who can easily spend hours if not days in my head, fantasizing and manifesting my ideal future. I've recognized my pattern of behavior and realized that the combination of procrastination and daydreaming is detrimental to my success in life, as well as for my overall well-being.

After months of studying, researching, and modeling highly successful people who reached the top of their respective professions, I began to notice certain patterns. They too struggle just like I do. Just like you do. Just like any other human being on the planet earth.

What separates them from the rest of society is the system they have in place, including mindset, habits and rituals.

To understand Joe's work ethic and discipline, firstly, you have to understand Joe Rogan himself. By now, you already have an idea of what makes him tick and what makes him do the things he does, regardless of their magnitude and regardless of how he comes across externally to the outside world.

> *I am a grinder. I get up every morning and I grind. People think you have to have a vision board to get started. I keep my head down and grind and when the time comes I just decide If I want to keep doing it.*
>
> *I want to get better.*
>
> *Workouts and things you don't want to do keep you grounded. They keep you routed in the reality of the struggle. I can not be happy if I am not struggling, I have to physically struggle or have mental challenges.*
>
> *Once I have that, I can be more appreciative of everything I have. I can be a more loving father, husband, friend. If you don't take care of your*

> *health, it's not just bad for you. It's bad for the people around you.*

Looking back at Joe Rogan's early life, it's hard not to notice the role of martial arts in his early adulthood, and more importantly, how martial arts and training made him into the machine that he is today. Joe spoke about it often and at length, in his JRE show and in many interviews he gave over the years.

As you can read from his quote above, Joe is a firm believer that without the appropriate challenge you can't truly be fulfilled as a being.

I have to physically struggle or have mental challenges.

In his famous rants, he often repeats his point on the importance of physical and mental challenges.

I don't know Joe personally and I couldn't attest to the moment Joe became aware of his beliefs. However, for the preparation and research, I have spent weeks immersed in the history, mind, circumstances, and context of Joe Rogan.
   One of the research aspects included was to listen to JRE show. (Truthfully, I have been watching JRE show consistently and often intensely since 2016)

In one specific episode with Jocko Willink, the two men talk about the meaning of discipline. In fact, Jocko is the perfect conversational partner for this topic. The former Navy SEAL and Navy officer, best-selling author, a successful entrepreneur and BJJ black belt.

Jocko is the real deal.

Although these two men come from very different environments and backgrounds, it's obvious how the sense of self-control and discipline lead to their success. Understandably so, Jocko is a man who spent most of his life in a military where exceptional discipline is required and non-negotiable. In fact, by his own admission, Jocko was a troublesome young man and he joined the navy because he felt he needed discipline.

Unlike Jocko who was in a military system where discipline is a given, the origin of Joe Rogan's work ethic is wildly different.

Since the age of 15, Joe became aware of the importance of hard work through martial arts training. Moreover, Joe realized just how much he can achieve when he puts his mind to something that truly interests him. With each and every accomplishment, Joe's belief around the importance of discipline got stronger, more powerful, and more self-serving.

Joe's first rewards and success came from his martial arts training.

After just a couple of years of training taekwondo, Joe became so proficient at it that he earned a position of a teacher, which was his job for a few years while he was pursuing a stand-up comedy career.

When it comes to his stand-up career and the value of discipline, it's easy to notice just how much it helped him reach the extraordinary level of success. Starting in 1988, Joe started developing a habit that will eventually lead him to where he is today — the position of one of the most influential people on the internet.

The habit was quite simple but it was absolutely necessary to develop considering his determination to reach the top of the stand-up comedy world. Joe Rogan began to write every day. At first, he wrote bits and jokes for his routine but later on, he began putting his thoughts down on paper.

Additionally, we have to address another activity that has been a part of Joe's life since early adulthood — **Physical Training.**

We've touched upon his martial arts background and beginnings in taekwondo, but his physical training goes well beyond that. Joe is a man famous for his intensive workout sessions and he is an advocate of *"breaking a sweat"* first thing in the morning. His advice to anyone who might be struggling in life is to start exercising and, ideally, do so in the morning.

From the biology standpoint, his advice is on point, as we know that after a workout, the body releases a hormone called endorphin.

Endorphins are amino acid sequences that work as neurotransmitters. Their production originates in the hypothalamus and the pituitary gland. Spicy food or chocolates, being in love, or feelings of excitement may also produce endorphins.

When we exercise, several processes occur in our bodies and minds that are of great benefit. For example, **blood flow increases, toxins are eliminated, muscle mass increases** and of course **endorphins are released.**

Although, you've probably heard of it and undoubtedly experienced its benefits, once you fully understand the power of this hormone and how to strategically use and manipulate it — It can be a game-changer.

For that reason, working out first thing in the morning set the tone for the rest of the day. Many personal development teachers and credible experts in their fields believe that seizing the day starts with dominating the morning. Even Joe Rogan who isn't a personal development guru believes that the first hour of your day is your *prime time.*

Understanding the importance of prime time and how to utilize the first hour of the day will be a needle mover into any direction of your choosing.

Why is discipline important and why having it is paramount to success in life?

"I am the laziest disciplined person I know" —*Joe Rogan*

In more than one of his podcast episodes or interviews, Joe talks about the importance of discipline. Moreover, he talks about the value of discipline and how his life looks like as a result. Before we get any further with a concrete manner of implementing a discipline in your life, ask yourself and subsequently answer the question:

"Why do I need to have discipline in my life?"

The answer to the question of why something truly matters to you will give you the necessary motivation to keep going. More importantly, knowing what you want in life and why will provide you with clarity and direction. There is a solid chance that you already know the answer to this question and it's just a matter of saying it out loud and accepting it.

When it comes to a matter of discipline, many are relying purely on the motivation element to get things done. Contrary to popular belief and self-help guru advice, motivation is just a good feeling in a body that makes us excited about a particular thing. Like any other feeling, motivation is fickle and fleeting and can't be relied on in the long run.

Usually, motivation is something people seek out externally.

Whether it's by watching an inspirational video on Youtube, a TED talk, reading a book, joining a community of like-minded people, or by visiting a personal development conference or event. While all of these things can help us feel invincible, inspired, and motivated to tackle the world, external motivation is not sustainable in the long run.

What is sustainable and prerequisite for your discipline is realizing that being motivated means having a strong reason to do something. The only sustainable motivation is the one that comes from the inside — *Intrinsic motivation.*

Regardless of the mountain you decided to conquer, tapping into the intrinsic motivation will be fuel for your journey.

In other words, discipline comes as a result of a decision to change. Change the old pattern of behavior and the beliefs that got you here but won't get you to where you want to be, and live the life you want to live.

You are the only one who can honestly and truthfully answer the question:

"What is my reason to change?"

For any change to be effective and for you to follow through, the decision behind the change has to resonate with you on a core level of your being. In other words, you should be emotionally invested in the potential outcome and not just resonate with a decision purely on the logical and rational level.

Just like Nietzsche *said: "When you have the 'WHY' for living, you can endure almost ANYHOW"*

In case you are having difficulties digging deeper and finding your 'WHY', I would encourage you to complete the exercise from the previous chapter. Knowing who you are, what you stand for, and what you believe in will help you find your answer.

However...

Even if you don't have a 'why' right now or you can't answer the above questions, it's not the end of the road or a reason to quit. The only answer that matters is always in the action, and as long as you keep going regardless of how you feel about it, it's a win.

For now, please, keep reading as we are about to break down the elusive force of discipline into a step-by-step process that anyone could easily follow.

'Just F*cking Do It!' is the worst advice to follow

We've already touched upon JRE episode with Jocko Willink where the two of them talk about the meaning of discipline. At one point during the conversation, Jocko said that *"Discipline equals Freedom. That's not a contradiction — it's an equation"*.

Discipline might appear to be the opposite of freedom. But, in fact, discipline is the path to freedom. Discipline is the driver of daily execution. Discipline defeats the infinite excuses that hold us back.

If one of your core values is freedom, you might be surprised to know just how spot-on Jocko's point is. There is no other way to freedom but discipline.

Success and failures are generally slow processes.

Just like an overnight success is a myth, the same should be said for a failure in life. It doesn't happen overnight. Both success and failure are the direct results and consequences of our daily actions, and choices we make.

Discipline is hard and it's difficult to sustain, regardless of where you are on your journey. Some of the most successful people, entrepreneurs, artists, athletes who have achieved a tremendous level of success are struggling to maintain discipline, just like you and me. What they do differently is going through the motion, regardless of they feel about it.

They've figured out a way to negotiate with themselves and do what has to be

49

done.

Just like Joe Rogan says: "Just fucking do it".

Joe is absolutely right as the solution is always in the action. Regardless of the area of your life you want to improve, there is no other way of doing so without consistent action.

Although it sounds simple it's far from being easy. The truth is much more nuanced than the 'Just Do It' solution. Moreover, the 'Just Do It' approach is more dangerous than it might seem on the surface.

When it comes to developing a discipline, many people fall into a trap of wanting to do too much too soon. Once they feel motivated enough, they will decide to do all the things they've been putting off for so long.

For example, they will decide to work out every day for an hour, they might start playing and practicing the guitar for another hour. In addition, they could decide to sign up for the local martial arts classes and take up an online course to finally learn how to create a profitable online business.

If this sounds like an exaggeration, I guarantee — it's not. As a matter of fact, this was my list of goals the first time I've decided to change my life around.

Can you guess what happened?

Nothing. I fell off the wagon a few weeks later. I did start off very strong as I went to the gym, practiced the guitar, and consumed a few courses on the topic of creating an online business. As if that wasn't enough, I also started with my kick-boxing sessions every other day. On top of all that, I had a full-time job and would often have to work overtime and over the weekends.

Little did I know back then, but willpower alone is not enough when it comes to developing a discipline. Moreover, willpower is a finite resource. Just like a battery, the more you use it, the more it drains until it's completely empty.

Sure enough, before I knew it, I've started slacking off in all areas of my desired improvements. Firstly, I ditched a guitar, then my kick-boxing practice. A couple of weeks later, I've put my online courses and classes on hold. Finally, I've stopped going to the gym and working out altogether.

My desire to tackle the world on my way to self-improvement fizzled out until it completely faded away.

The worst part? I felt like crap. Physically, mentally and emotionally. I felt like a failure, which I was. However, that failure provided me with a learning experience that changed my outlook on the entire personal development matter.

The key learning point is that you can't do it all at once.

Personal development is done through small incremented steps and habits. One day at a time, one step at a time. Focusing on one or two small changes done daily will inevitably lead to a snowball effect. Once those small changes become a part of your daily routine, you can start implementing new habits.

Years later I've started studying and observing highly successful people from all walks of life. Sure enough, when it comes to developing a world-class discipline and implementing habits, they have a similar approach.

* * *

How To Develop a World-Class Discipline Model

1) Find Your Challenge

As Joe Rogan said: *"**I have to physically struggle or have mental challenges.**"*

Just like Joe believes that fitness and writing are the cornerstones for his success, so do I. As a matter of fact, my life transformed once I implemented two regular daily habits. Fitness and Journaling. Truthfully, I've exercised and journaled before, especially in my early twenties. However, for one reason or another, I've never made it a consistent habit.

Once I've decided to commit and use this simple model I am about to share with you, my life changed because I did.

Maybe you already have things in the back of your head you want to improve and incorporate into your daily life. Even if that is the case, I wholeheartedly recommend listening to Joe Rogan's simple advice for improvement and success: *Physical struggle and mental challenge.*

Still, before you take his advice at face value, it's important to acknowledge your starting point. When it comes to your fitness, be honest with yourself about where you are at the moment.

If you never exercised before, it would be insane to go to the gym and bench press 300lbs. In the same way, it would be crazy to go for a 5 mile run if the last time you did so was in high school. Even if you could do it, the next day or maybe the entire week would be a living hell, which in turn would probably make you quit.

The goal is to get progressively better. Over time, you'll raise your fitness level but keep in mind that requires patience and more importantly—Consistency.

Regardless of your starting point, take a steady approach.

For the first week, go for a light jog or simply walk around your neighborhood. Before you sign up for the local gym, start with home-based workouts. A gym can be an overwhelming experience for anyone who never stepped foot inside before.

However, if you are a hardcore person deep inside, go for it immediately. Especially, if you are not a complete beginner or you have a few years of training under your belt. Even if that is the case, remember to take it slowly at the beginning as your body adjusts to a sudden change and physical stress.

As the physical aspect of your being improves, you will notice a mental clarity you haven't had before. (or it's been so long that you forgot how it looks like and feels like)

For that reason, the other challenge that goes hand in hand with your fitness is *journaling.*

The whole point of the exercise is to develop a 'writing muscle' which is nothing more than a habit in place. Keeping a journal is great for a variety of reasons. Aside from the writing itself, you keep track of your life.

Just like the internet archive and Wayback machine, a few years from now, you can see exactly where you were at any given moment. All it takes is a few paragraphs to see the past for how it really was. You can use the information and past experience, as you look to the future for that whichever comes next.

Many people I've personally met and spent some time with, use journaling in a therapeutic manner. Many of those people are coaches and psychologists and recommend the same treatment for their patients and clients.

The same advice and approach you take for your fitness, apply for journaling, too. Take it slow but do it every day. If you never journaled before, and you have no idea where and how to start, write about whatever comes to mind at that moment.

After the first few paragraphs, what really matters will come to the forefront of your consciousness. You can write about your day, your training, work or anything else. The only rule for keeping a journal is that there are absolutely no rules at all.

The initial reason for starting is irrelevant. What truly matters is that you start and persist. After a short while, you will see the direct rewards from the action of writing. Your thoughts will become clear, new ideas might emerge from somewhere in the aether. (Maybe even from you and your subconscious mind).

Don't be surprised if you realize a few crucial things along the way, those 'Aha' moments that come seemingly out of nowhere.

After a while, you won't feel these two actions like a chore and something you have to do. On the contrary, you will look forward to the action of writing and exercising because of the feeling that comes afterward. The priceless feeling of accomplishment as you build yourself on your way to success.

Before we conclude this point, I have to emphasize the following:

Fitness and journaling are just my suggestion based on my personal experience, and also, based on Joe Rogan's success model. You don't have to do it, especially if you already have something that speaks to you from deep inside.

Whatever you decide and chose to start with:
Remember to trust the process and to trust yourself.

2. Make the Challenge Your AA

Firstly, what does AA stand for?

Anchor Action.

We live in a fast-paced world full of all kinds of DDL, responsibilities, and to-do lists. It's understandable why it's easy to neglect our own well-being and fail to take care of ourselves.

Because of that, in today's day and age, it's crucial to have something to fall back on, to keep you centered and connected with your true self.

This is your anchor action.

Just like a ship that needs a powerful anchor to prevent it from drifting away due to strong winds or a current, so do the highly successful people from all walks of life.

As mentioned before, Joe Rogan's anchor actions are physical exercise and writing. Besides a fact that he is arguably the biggest star in Hollywood, Dwayne 'The Rock' Johnson is renowned for his 4 AM workouts. Another movie star, Mathew McConaughey is a firm believer in 'breaking a sweat' first thing in the morning.

Although the above-mentioned examples are about physical training, it doesn't have to be only about working out. On the contrary, some find their anchor in meditation, taking a walk in nature, playing an instrument, journaling, spending time with their loved ones and children...

You are the only one responsible for creating your anchor. No one in the world can and should tell you what is your anchor action. You are the captain of your ship and you choose the anchor.

There is only one rule you need to adhere to if you want to succeed: **Your anchor action is non-negotiable.**

In other words, you have to do it. Every single day. As much as I dislike and don't believe in the absolutes like 'have to', this is the one exception all successful people know. There is no other way around it, but to go through with it.

Because we live in a hectic world full of all kinds of distractions, it's easy to fall into the trap of making excuses. We, humans, are rationalizing machines and we can easily buy into those rationalizations.

For this reason, it's important to adopt the appropriate perspective and view these simple daily actions as your anchor. For others, it might seem silly that your daily meditation practice means so much, but for you, it should be the most important thing throughout the day — a matter of life or death.

Because, when everything else fails and life seems to hit you hard over and over again, you will find your solace in your anchor action. In your anchor action, you will find inner peace, you will ground yourself and be ready to take on the world, regardless of what it throws at you.

3. Utilize Your Prime Time

We've touched upon the notion of prime time earlier, but let's expand on the idea and see how to utilize it. Quite simply, prime time is the first hour after waking up, and the last hour before you go to sleep. The moment you wake up, you are arguably at your peak state and you are 'untainted' by the external world.

Allow me to explain further.

Unfortunately, for many people nowadays the first thing they do is check their phone. Some do it because of work, and all the urgent emails from their boss, colleague, or client. Others do it to check on social media, see how many likes they've got from last night's post.

Unfortunately, most do it because of the power of habit. Regardless of the reason, the end result is the same. They are robbing themselves of an opportunity to start the day on a high note.

Before you check in with the world, check in with yourself first.

Once we engage with the external world through technology and social media, we are influenced both on the conscious but also on the subconscious level.

Opening an email 10 minutes after waking up and seeing an urgent message from a client about the screw-up on the project will most certainly put you in an alert and anxious state of being. You will undoubtedly put all of your energy and focus into solving the problem. Even if you manage to solve the problem right away, you will do so at the expense of yourself because you've set the tone for the rest of the day.

Conversely, starting your day by scrolling through Instagram and seeing your college buddy traveling the world and seemingly enjoying life will undoubtedly put a seed of doubt into your subconscious mind. That seed will grow until at one point, it manifests in the conscious mind as a random thought.

Random thought that your life maybe isn't good enough and that you are not good enough. (If you think this is an exaggeration, please watch the documentary ''Social Dilemma''. You will see all of the manipulative tactics social media platforms use to essentially modify human behavior)

The same principle applies to prime time in the evening. Because we are so addicted to technology, we are even taking it to bed as we mindlessly scroll through the feed. The last hour of the evening should be all about unwinding and relaxing in the comfort of your home, ideally with your loved one.

So...what should you do instead?

Firstly, realize the power and the utmost importance of your prime time. If you are deliberate about your personal growth, you have to start investing in yourself. In an ideal world and scenario, the first hour of the day, as well as the last one before you go to sleep, should be all about you. No technology, no external influences. Just you and your thoughts.

Unfortunately, for one reason or another, most of us don't have the luxury of the ideal scenario. We live in the 'real' world where life happens and we have to adjust. However, we have more control over our lives than we think.

If you can't have the first hour of the day for yourself for prime time, then use *anytime as your prime time.* Anytime you can take a break from work or family responsibilities will be good enough. It doesn't have to be a full hour but use as much as you possibly can and do your *Anchor Action.*

Remember: On your way to success, your Anchor Action is non-negotiable.

4. Don't Break the Chain Life Hack

Years ago there was a man named Brad Isaac. Brad was a young comedian just starting out on the comedy circuit. One night, he found himself in the same comedy club as Jerry Seinfeld. (Yes, that Seinfeld)

Eager to meet his hero, Brad took the opportunity to approach Seinfeld before the show and ask for advice to become a better comedian. What legendary Seinfeld shared with young Brad is one of the most brilliant productivity hacks. This simple hack is a gem of a leverage technique he used on himself and you can use it to motivate yourself — even when you don't feel like it.

Years later, Brad shared his story with LifeHacker magazine.

> *''He said the way to be a better comic was to create better jokes and the way to create better jokes was to write every day.*
>
> *He told me to get a big wall calendar that has a whole year on one page and hang it on a prominent wall. The next step was to get a big red magic marker. He said for each day that I do my task of writing, I get to put a big red X over that day.*
>
> *"After a few days you'll have a chain. Just keep at it and the chain will grow longer every day. You'll like seeing that chain, especially when you get a few weeks under your belt. Your only job is to not break the chain."*

It's remarkable to think that a simple method like this one shaped one of the greatest and most successful comedians of all time.

Jerry Seinfeld is regarded as one of the "Top 100 Comedians of All-Time" by Comedy Central. He was also the co-creator and co-writer of *Seinfeld*, the long-running sitcom which has received numerous awards and was claimed to have the "Top TV Episode of All-Time" as rated by *TV Guide*. According to *Forbes* magazine, Seinfeld reached his peak in earnings when he made $267 million dollars in 1998.

In other words..."Don't Break the Chain" method works.

It's not a secret that building or removing any habit requires patience and consistency. For that reason, many fail to do so, and sooner or later they fall off the wagon. Unfortunately, most never get back on that wagon as they accept that change is impossible.

To make a permanent change in life, it has to come from deep inside. The change has to happen on the identity level, rather than purely on the surface. For any change to happen on that identity level, it has to mean something to you and you have to actually want to change and improve as a result.

A dear friend of mine struggled for years to quit smoking.

He would try over and over again but after a while, he would return to his old habits. As it turned out eventually, he didn't really want to quit. As a matter of fact, it was his wife that wanted him to quit smoking and live a healthier lifestyle.

The only leverage you'll ever need in a battle of creating a habit and being disciplined is the one you create for yourself. Maybe you've tried to implement a new habit in your life, and you've failed to make that habit stick permanently.

If that is the case, why should now be any different?

Because, now, you have the right system to follow through rather than a pure desire and will to change.

On its own, even the *'Don't Break the Chain'* method probably won't work. However, when you take time to introspect on your life and realize your values, before committing—the odds are heavily stacked in your favor.

Furthermore, once you establish a challenge that is aligned with those values, make it your *AA and utilize your Prime Time, the ''Don't Break the Chain''* method becomes even more potent and powerful.

How to replicate the 'Don't Break the Chain' method in your life?

As you read from Brad Isaac's quote above, the actual method is quite simple and straightforward.

Firstly, get a physical calendar and put it in a prominent place. Somewhere where you will have to see it regularly. If you can't find an old-fashioned calendar, make one yourself. Get a big piece of paper and mark the days, months and if possible, the entire year.

Secondly, get a red marker. Any other color will do the job but there is something uniquely satisfying when you see a chain of red X.

Thirdly, every time you do your Anchor Action, put a big red X over that date.

As Jerry Seinfeld told a young comedian, after few weeks you will want to see the chain grow further and further. Even when you don't feel like doing your AA, I guarantee you'll go the extra mile just to keep the chain 'alive.'

Important note: If you choose fitness and working out as your anchor, you will have to have your rest days. On your day off from the gym, simply take a walk in nature and enjoy that rest day. You can still mark the day with a big red X.

Alternatively, you could go completely digital and use an app Chains.cc. Truthfully, I've never used it but according to online reviews and comments, it seems reliable and a decent solution for those who've used it.

Now that you have a system and a direction, I wish you all the luck in the world on your journey. The journey of building a world-class discipline and self-mastery. The road will be long and it won't be a walk in the park. You will doubt yourself and your decision to embark on the journey but in the end — It will be worth it.

Keep in mind that small wins accumulate into major improvements over time. Consistent action will inevitably result in compounding interest.

5

Charisma

"When someone comes along and expresses him or herself as freely as they think, people flock to it. They enjoy it." – Joe Rogan

Every dialogue by nature is a conversation, while the opposite can't be said for each and every conversation. Unfortunately, a conversation doesn't necessarily mean dialogue, and often, it's not. Although we hear it constantly, a dialogue is the only way for us to move forward as a civilization.

In light of everything that has happened in the last few years, the rift and a division between people seem larger than ever before.

Genuine dialogue is a middle ground for understanding each other. It's a place where every party involved is heard and their point of view is acknowledged.

For many of the JRE guests coming over to the show means they are recognized in their respective fields. It also means additional exposure with millions of fans watching every episode. Some see it as an opportunity for self-promotion, but many come over to the show because they know they can expect one thing from Joe Rogan.

They know that they will be heard, acknowledged and that a dialogue is guaranteed.

Joe Rogan Experience isn't a typical podcast. Unlike any other show on the internet or television, a typical JRE show duration is around between two and three hours. Regardless of the guest on the show, each conversation between Joe and that guest is fascinating and captivating. In today's day and age holding the attention of your audience for that long seems almost like a miracle.

What is Joe Rogan's secret and how does he do that?

The answer is simple and it isn't much of a secret at all. Joe Rogan's charisma is a major factor for the show's success and a reason why so many high-profile guests come over again and again.

In this chapter, we'll focus on the elusive topic of charisma and break down Joe Rogan's charisma style. For some reason, charisma seems to be shrouded with a veil of mystery as no one can really pinpoint the exact ingredient you need to have to be charismatic.

As Bruce Lee famously said: *"Simplicity is the key to brilliance"*

In deconstructing the matter of charisma, there is absolutely no need to overcomplicate. To put it simply, in its essence, *charisma is the result of exceptional communication and interpersonal skills.*

When it comes to the charisma and personality aspect of an individual, the question inevitable boils down to:

"Are you born with an incredible gift that is charisma; or is charisma something you develop later on in life?"

Essentially, what we are looking at here is the eternal question of *nature vs nurture. Are we born this way or are we a product of our environment and life circumstances?*

Many clinical psychiatrists, scientists and researchers will agree that most likely the combination of two plays a critical factor in the formation of a personality.

Bruce Lipton, a developmental biologist known for his work in epigenetic and cell biology, caused quite a stern in scientific circles with his book ''The Biology of Belief'', in which he claimed that belief control human biology rather than DNA and inheritance. According to Lipton, the conscious mind can learn in a variety of ways, while the subconscious mind learns in two fundamental ways:

1. Through hypnosis
2. Through repetition

Through the first seven years of their existence, children, mostly, learn unconsciously. As we grow, we exhibit the patterns of behavior that we've picked up unconsciously. As an example of this idea, based on the studies and researches we now have available, we know that children of a sociopath will most likely become one as they grow up.

Once we are all grown up, the only way to learn is through practice and repetition. Learning how to play an instrument requires hours and hours of repetitive practice. The same can be said for any other skill we wish to pick up, including charisma which essentially is a combination of interpersonal skills.

What does the nature vs nurture argument have to do with Joe Rogan and his charisma?

Some of Joe's earliest memories are of his abusive and angry father. Luckily for Joe and the rest of the society, his mother moved away from her husband and later remarried to a man who provided her and little Joe with a proper home. Joe often speaks about the harmony, love, and support he received while growing up.

Joe remembers how the culture of dialogue, listening, and understanding was prevalent in his household while describing his mom and stepfather as *"people full of love and support"*. However, just because Joe was fortunate enough to grow up in a loving family isn't the only reason for his undeniable charisma.

Over the years, Joe has picked up on certain communication skills elements that make him an incredible conversationalist.

The first element of charisma we are going to cover and the one Joe excels at is...

The Subtle Art of Small Talk

There are a few things we as humanity dread more than the small talk. Many chose not to engage in a conversation at all, just to avoid the pain of going through the small talk.

For many, the real issue is the perception of small talk. They perceive it as a necessity, instead of an opportunity. Because of that perception, the actual small talk will inevitably feel like a chore.

However, there are those seemingly gifted individuals who relish the opportunity to strike up the conversation with a relative stranger. They seem to be the life of every party as they magically work any room they find themselves in. It's a pure joy to watch them form instant connections with people around them.

I am sure you already have someone in mind who fits the description above.

So, what are those gifted charismatic individuals doing differently?

Firstly, they see the mandatory small for what it really is. *They know that the only purpose of small talk is to provide a gateway to a more meaningful conversation, and eventually a deeper connection between people.*

Additionally, those with an undeniable charisma approach the small talk with the following attitude:

1) They know the difference between small talk and trivial talk.
    The trivial talk is the one that leads nowhere, and no actual value has been exchanged in the interaction. Instead, this chatter is just noise that you will forget the moment the talk ends.
    2) They give sincere compliments
    The easiest way to start a conversation has to be the one that starts with a sincere compliment. Over the years, I have noticed many of my female friends and acquaintances doing this to absolute perfection. Generally speaking, women have a much higher perception threshold than men. In other words, an average woman notices much more than her male counterpart. Acknowledging something you like or appreciate about another person can go a long way toward establishing an instant rapport with them.

3)They are comfortable with the silence
    Those who enjoy and thrive in small talk are the same people who are comfortable with silence. They don't force the small talk for the sake of avoiding an uncomfortable silence. If they don't have anything valuable to offer to another person, they will keep quiet. Sometimes, and especially as the conversation progress, that conversation needs to 'breathe'.
    In those moments of silence, each party has to process and what was just said. A great conversationalist recognizes those moments and gives others space and time to do so, because forcing a conversation in those moments can

only be counterproductive.

After watching countless of JRE episodes on Youtube, I have to conclude that Joe Rogan does all of the above things to absolute perfection. It's almost magical to see the staggering difference between the beginning of the show and the ending.

Some of Joe's guests who come to the show for the first time are notably reserved at first, but Joe's ability to lead the conversation and allow the guest to fully express themselves is remarkable. It's incredible to witness their transformation by the end of the show.

We mentioned above the importance of distinguishing trivial talk from small talk. Joe does this brilliantly and he keeps things simple during the initial stage of the conversation. In all fairness, Joe has leverage on us, mere mortals.

Unlike most of us who meet someone for the first time, Joe has some knowledge or prior information about his guest. At the very least, Joe Rogan is aware of the potential conversational avenues he can take at any moment, or even transition into during the conversation.

For the most part, when we first meet someone at a party, social gathering, or networking event, without that prior information about the other person, we don't have anything to fall back on during the conversation.

Because of that reason, if we actually want to meet a person in front, we have to start from scratch. Oftentimes, starting from scratch means exchanging the most common questions when meeting someone for the first time.

Almost exclusively, those questions are:

1. Where are you from?
2. What do you do for a living?

There is nothing inherently wrong with these questions but once answered the conversation usually hits the dead-end as the dreaded awkward silence occurs. As a matter of fact, contrary to popular belief, these questions are ideal conversation starters as they are non-invasive in their essence.

For example:

"Where are you from?"

"I am from Mount Pleasant, Michigan. "

"Awesome! If I were to travel there tomorrow, what would you say is a must-experience thing in Mount Pleasant?"

You've just opened an entire conversational avenue. However the other person chooses to respond, now you have something to talk about. The easiest way to proceed from here is to ask a simple question that goes one layer deeper.

"Hm..Why?"

Now, you are on the way to learning more about their motivation, values, and character traits.

The 'trick' during the initial stages of the interaction, and when engaging in small talk, is to lead the conversation from facts and statements to feelings and stories as soon as possible.

The Power of Storytelling

The ability to tell stories is a crafty skill to have in your charisma arsenal.

In fact, we relate to each other through stories and have been since the beginning of humanity. For as long as stories existed, they have been intertwined with emotions and feelings. A good story can move and uplift us, inspire us, make us joyous, happy, or scared.

A great story makes you feel.

Stand-up comedians tell stories to make us laugh. They are exceptional at telling stories.

In fact, Joe Rogan is a master storyteller. As a comedian, he had to learn how to tell funny stories on stage and make people laugh. He wasn't born with this skill, and Joe remembers his first stand-up show to be an awful experience for both him and the audience.

However, Joe, just like every other great standup comedian, tries new material in front of a small audience first. They tell the stories and based on the reception, tweak it and test again. By the time, we get to see them live or in their new special, they've mastered those stories. They've told them and practiced so many times, they could do it in their sleep.

If there is a formula for getting good and exceptional at something, it would be just a simple reminder:

Consistency+Dedication+Patience = Mastery

In addition to Joe's ability to tell stories on stage and make people laugh, he is also a master of storytelling in a private setting, like in his JRE studio, to an audience of one.

When it comes to storytelling and especially getting good at telling them in a smaller circle of people, the same reminder applies. Unlike telling a story on a stage to a large audience of people, sharing a story to a few people is a lot more intimate experience. The one that brings people together.

The best example I found while researching potential topics for this book, would have to be an episode of JRE with Kevin Smith.

Kevin is an American filmmaker, actor, comedian, comic book writer, author, and podcaster. He came to prominence with the low-budget comedy film *Clerks* (1994), which he wrote, directed, co-produced, and acted in as the character Silent Bob of stoner duo Jay and Silent Bob.

Kevin is also a fantastic conversationalist and in this particular episode, both Joe and Kevin shared their personal stories. In one particular segment of the show, both men talked about their love for animals and especially their dogs.

Joe told a story of a sick puppy he adopted and unfortunately had to put down. It's obvious that Joe hasn't rehearsed this story and that he was remembering it as he told it. Nonetheless, both Joe and Kevin had a teary eye by the end of the story.

On the other hand, Kevin shared a story of his two yellow labradors, properly named Scully and Mulder.

Interestingly, while telling a story Kevin takes a listener through the roller-coaster of emotions. In the beginning, he talks about the time he met them and how adorable and funny they were as puppies.

As the story went on, and the inevitable end is near, Kevin remembers how difficult it was to witness their last hours before passing away. Needless to say, both men shared a tear and inevitably bonded over their similar life experiences.

How to find your story?

There isn't an environment where a story doesn't elevate the experience. When you tell a well-crafted story, it unlocks the feeling of intimacy in others, as they relate to you and your story.

The content is important as it provides the information, but a well-crafted and properly delivered story is the bridge that connects us on a deeper level.

The language you use is shaping your life experiences, and your experience is shaping your life story. For that reason, think about those life experiences that shaped you into the person you are today.

Your stories are already there and are disguised as moments in time. If you don't know where to look for a good story — *start with your childhood.*

Remember how easy it was to tell stories when you were a child. Kids are natural storytellers. Unlike us, the adults, children are not confined by social rules and norms. They don't think or analyze the situation too much, if at all.

Maybe the most admirable children characteristic is their mindset about the world around them. Kids have this innate ability to take the most trivial everyday experience and make the most memorable story out of it.

They are curious, fearless, and playful little creatures. They, also, bring those same qualities when telling a story. Allow yourself to tap into your inner child and try observing the world through the eyes of a child.

Maybe your most memorable stories are from your early adulthood, college, or your current job.

However, before you start telling stories, most importantly...

Start with an end in mind

What does a win for your listener look like?

Unless you are at a job interview where you only have one chance to impress the interviewer, you should be speaking to inspire not to impress. Speak to inspire a particular action, speak to inspire a particular feeling, speak to inspire a particular awareness.

Anytime you are about to tell a story, ask yourself:

- What is the purpose of this story?
- Why am I telling this story?
- How does the story end?
- How do I want to make others feel once I finish the story?

The idea behind answering the first three questions upfront is simple.

Think about it: You *create and control the narrative of your story* by knowing what's the purpose of that story, how it ends, and why are you telling it.

Answering the last question can allow you to relate with people and resonate with them on a much deeper level. Causing others to feel good while in your company and enjoying listening to you is one of the most generous gifts you can give them. In return, you will enjoy telling stories even more.

Start with an end in mind even if it's just a casual story because the last thing you want is to make people feel drab or confused.

A few years ago, I have worked on a specific project. The only reason why I even remember that project is because of my colleague. He was the uncrowned champion of telling the most mundane and trivial stories based on his everyday existence.

On many occasions, I've tried to focus and even participate in a conversation. But it wasn't a conversation — it was a monologue. A monologue that varied in duration but was fairly consistent in intensity, as every story he told carried the intense dull sensation. The stories definitely had potential but the way he delivered them always left me confused by the end.

As much as I've enjoyed working with him, as he was an exceptional talent and a professional, hanging out with him outside of work became unbearable and I've started avoiding him.

So to avoid getting people to avoid you — start with an end in mind, create and control the narrative of your stories.

Simply, ask yourself a question:
   "How do I want to make them feel by the end of this story?"

The Untold Truth of Listening and Facilitating

Joe Rogan has another powerful weapon in his charisma arsenal.

He is incredible at facilitating conversation. Facilitation is a skill often associated with great leaders and managers, but it can be so much more than that.

Facilitation is about helping others process an issue or idea. When people reach a conclusion through their own thought process, the result is far more impactful than if they act on someone else's ideas. Unlike a public speaker or a presenter, a facilitator is a person who willingly allows the other person to shine in the spotlight.

A great facilitator will carefully listen and ask questions to guide the conversation and the other person towards important realizations or conclusions.

Therefore, the first and crucial step before you begin to facilitate the interaction, you have to actually listen. In fact, listening and facilitation go hand in hand. Although it sounds like common sense, actually listening to another person requires a substantial effort on our part.

Unfortunately, listening isn't something we intuitively and naturally do, like breathing or blinking. In reality, during a conversation, many confuse hearing with listening. Most people, most of the time, are just waiting for their turn to speak.

When it comes to listening, if your goal is to connect with the person in front of you, there are a few rules or rather a framework you should adopt and follow through.

1. Focus on Learning and Understanding

Before any interaction, the most important thing to have is the right mindset. The mindset of learning and understanding rather than merely replying and waiting for your turn to talk.

In most cases, people don't need a good talking to, but a good listening to.

Having this in the back of your head will help you steer the conversation in the desired direction. A direction of learning about the other person. Whenever possible, steer the conversation towards feelings rather than pure facts.

Learning about the other person's motivation in life and the reason they do the things they do will allow you to gain an insight into their character. To do that, adopt and nurture the attitude of curiosity.

We've already touched upon the children and how they approach the subject of storytelling. Aside from being natural storytellers, kids are excellent at getting to the root cause of things, by asking a simple question of *"Why?"*

As a matter of fact, the Five whys (or **5 whys**) is an iterative interrogative technique used to explore the cause-and-effect relationships underlying a particular problem. The primary goal of the technique is to determine the root cause of a defect or problem by repeating the question "Why?".

Each answer forms the basis of the next question.

The "five" in the name derives from an anecdotal observation on the number of iterations needed to resolve the problem. This is a technique effectively used in corporate environments and company meetings, but it can be effectively replicated in everyday life and regular social interactions.

More often than not, to get to the root cause of a problem or someone's motivation in life, you don't need to ask all of the 5 whys. Sometimes, people will open up as soon as you ask the first ''why?'', and your only job is to pay close attention to what they are actually saying.

For that reason, it's crucial to...

2. Give Your Undivided Attention

One of the greatest gifts you can give to others is your attention, regardless of the situation or circumstances. Whether you've just met someone or you're having a casual conversation with a friend.

Many people think body language is a crucial factor in any interaction. While it's important to practice open body language during a conversation, the act alone will not magically connect you with a person in front of you.

One thing we should keep in mind is that a body is and always will be a servant of the mind. In other words, if your intention is to learn about others, you will display open body language and send a message to the other person that you're listening.

Instead of focusing on all the body language techniques you have to use, and putting them in the right sequence, here is one thing every one of us can easily achieve. It's something you should never do in a conversation.

For whatever reason, don't use your phone when talking to another person.

Nothing kills the connection between two people quicker than a smartphone. I am baffled by the number of people who do this on the regular basis.

Taking out your phone sends a powerful message that something else is more important than the ongoing interaction. In the case of an emergency, politely excuse yourself. Otherwise, Instagram notifications will still be there 10 minutes later. The same goes for that message you've received or urgent email just waiting for your response in the inbox.

As a rule of thumb, if you want to be interesting, you have to be interested first. Face to face interaction that is occurring in the very moment always comes before an online conversation (email, text message, notification, and even a phone call)

Even if the smartphone is out of the equation and out of sight, many of us have to deliberately focus while having a conversation. Due to the fast-paced nature of our lives, which has somehow become a norm nowadays, our attention is often scattered. More often than not, during the conversation, the mind will find a way to wonder of.

If you notice a similar occurrence, catch yourself as soon as you start 'drifting' away mid-conversation. It might require a conscious effort to do so, but it's always well worth it. Aside from being a gift to others, your undivided attention in the conversation is one of the best investments you can make for yourself.

Remember: The more attention, the more information.

3. Show That You Listen

When it comes to human interaction, active listening is one of the most important skills you can develop. The fastest way to show someone you are listening is to engage in a conversation by asking questions.

There are no right or wrong questions. Only those that work or don't work.

The questions that work are those that show your desire to learn more about the topic at hand. There are many techniques out there, but one of the most effective ones is called *"Linking"*.

It's all about repeating or rephrasing what the other person said previously and linking it with a follow-up question or a statement that validates and reinforces the related idea.

Doing this in an ongoing conversation sends a message to the other person — you are listening, and you care. Unfortunately, not many people leave that kind of impression. Even though the fastest way to learn is to ask questions, a conversation shouldn't be an interview.

So don't make it a series of "yes or no" questions, asked just for the sake of asking. Feel free to give your perspective and opinion to keep that conversation as dynamic as possible.

4. Hear the Meaning (Not the Words)

If you pay attention in a conversation, you will notice that different topics bring out a different emotion in the person you're talking to. Hear the meaning that drives those words. Once you do, stay on that course.

If possible, discover the real reason behind that feeling. Knowing what excites someone and why is valuable information you can use in forming social connections.

Remember those topics that invoked a positive emotional response from the other person.

You don't have to remember the entire conversation, just the highlights. Those highlights are topics that caused that emotion. Make a mental note in your head, because you are going to need it for the next and final step.

5. Follow up and Follow through (Connection Bridge Principle)

The last and often neglected step. Also, the crucial one, especially if you know that you are going to see that person again and that the previous conversation wasn't the last one.

This is one of the things Tom Cruise excels at (reportedly he learns the crew's names, treats everybody as an equal, and months later will remember to ask how their kids are doing.)
Let's face it.

No matter how good of an impression we made on someone, or how much someone liked us, a follow-up is a must.

People tend to forget. The more time passed between the conversations, the less likely will people remember how much you cared and how good you made them feel.

A connection bridge principle serves to reduce the gap from the last time we had a conversation with someone until the present moment. Use the highlight from the previous interaction to pick up where you left off.
   If the highlight of the conversation was about fitness us that as a conversation starter. Most of the time bringing up the previous highlight will bring the same positive emotion from the other person. .

It is also a great icebreaker, so you don't have to fall back on good old small talk.

* * *

As we already established, charisma is a combination of exceptional interpersonal and communication skills. Each and every one of us is unique in our essence. We are different from one another, and our communication style is unique to us.

Joe Rogan's charisma lies in his unique ability to facilitate any conversation, regardless of the social context. This is especially the case with his JRE show, where he provides a platform for his guests to express themselves. Joe is an incredible listener and facilitator, which is undoubtedly one of the reasons why his show achieved worldwide popularity and success.

Joe's charisma combined with his work ethic and his authenticity is the reason why he is winning in the game of life.

6

Final Words

"In all my travelings, all my life adventures; I have to say I still don't know what life is, absolutely no clue, and it is a subject that is constantly on my mind. One thing I do know for a fact is that the nicer we are to our fellow human beings, the nicer the universe is to us." – **Joe Rogan**

Success should be viewed as a continual process as life unfolds, instead of an outside element beyond our grasp. Success is not a blessing reserved for a chosen few. Success is our birthright, and it's up to each and every one of us to exercise that right as we purposefully design our lives.

In today's day and age, it's easy to be seduced by Hollywood's glamour or the success of various social media influencers who seemingly live the dream. It's easy to look around at those who are successful and say how amazing they are.

It's easy to do so because it lets you off the hook and a one-step from the crucial self-realization.

You are amazing, too. Just the way you are.

You are enough, and you have enough to succeed in the game of life. You already have all the resources you need to win the game of life. The only thing you may be missing is the clarity of a direction. Having clarity and a direction requires reaching deep down, and honestly answering the question:

What is success to me?

Success is a relative term, and it means different things to different people. To the CEO of a Fortune 500 company, success might be growing steadily in revenue and profit, year after year. To an independent writer and publisher, success means getting that one positive review on a book she worked so hard to produce. To a dedicated homemaker, success probably means that she has a wonderful family and a well-run household.

I have spent most of my adult life practicing personal development ideas and concepts. I came across countless definitions of success, but the one that deeply resonated with me was the one from a man who lived 150 years ago.

William James, one of the most notable philosophers and a man considered a "father of American psychology," described success as a combination of two things:

1. ***An inner ideal which is followed persistently with courage***
2. ***An outer achievement related to that ideal***

An ***inner ideal*** means defining a goal and having the resolve to complete it. Regardless of the size of the goal, cultivate the *"I'll figure it out, no matter what"* attitude and work on the goal until you succeed.

One of the biggest misconceptions and misinformation about success, especially in the personal development sphere, is the need to have a big picture of your life.

It's the false narrative "You gotta have a BIG WHY for life" partially created by internet marketers that flooded the personal development space over the last ten years, masqueraded as self-help gurus teaching you how to live your life.

Having a short-term goal is a great start.

Back in 1988, before he came upon the stage for his first show, Joe Rogan didn't know where exactly he will end up one day. Not even in his wildest dreams could he imagine that one day in the future, he will be a cultural icon and a role model to millions of people around the globe.

No.

The only thing Joe deeply cared about back then was his inner ideal. He loved stand-up comedy and he enjoyed making people laugh. His goal was to get better with each performance and to book the next show. Day by day, Joe Rogan diligently worked on his craft and relentlessly pursued his passion.

The second part of the success equation is quite simple: What can I showcase to the world?

What you showcase to the world is an *outer achievement*, and it has to be a tangible result of pursuing the inner ideal. I deeply believe that the inner ideal as a goal is to be hidden from the world. For the most part, people in this world essentially don't care because they are too busy dealing with their lives.

Those close to you will prefer action over another talk any given day, anyway.

Instead of telling the world what you are going to do, show them what you have done.

What gets you to your success destination is action, and once you get the momentum, your horizons will expand. New opportunities will be revealed to you, as a consequence and a result of your experience. You don't need to have all the answers up front. You just need to start.

As important as goals are for any individual, it's absolutely necessary to have a proper system that will get you to where you want to be. Joe Rogan's system for success includes empowering self-beliefs, consistent practice, daily rituals, and diligent work on his craft.

Maybe the most important element of his success system is his ability to create and develop deep and meaningful social connections, nurture and grow his relationships.

Ultimately, Joe's success story and his success models should only serve you as an inspiration and a guideline.

The value of life is having the free will to make up your own answers as you go along, including your answers on how to be successful and win the game of life.

If there was a single absolute answer, we absolutely wouldn't be free. We would be trapped in limbo, desperately trying to live up to that specific yet absolute answer as the only measure of success and victory.

Fortunately, the beauty of the mysterious nature of life is that there are no definitive answers. The magic lies in the act of pursuing the answers to great questions of life.

You are the hero of your own story.

Dare to dream big and follow your inner ideals. You are free to explore, live your most abundant life, forge your path and create your own models for success. If you do that...

You will win the game of life.

* * *

A personal note from the author:

In case you've enjoyed your experience with this book, please consider leaving a short review and a rating.

In case a short written review is too much to ask, you can simply rate the experience you feel describes your satisfaction with this book.

Log into Amazon, click on 'Your account', and then click on the 'Orders'. From your history of purchases, select this book and leave your rating.

It will only require about 45 seconds of your time. On the other hand, for an independent writer and publisher, your review and rating mean the world to me.

My dream is to reach a million readers and every single rating and a positive review brings me one step closer to that dream.

Regardless of your choice, I want to thank you from the bottom of my heart. Thank you for getting a copy of this book. I hope you've learned something new, gain insight or a nugget of wisdom.
    Until next time,
    Alex Karadzin

Gift For You

"Genius is one part inspiration and ninety-nine percent perspiration." –
Thomas Edison

And while there's no discounting the tremendous value of the perspiration, it's the inspiration that sets the wheels in motion.

But what exactly is Inspiration and why is it so important?

Although a fleeting feeling hard to pinpoint, you feel ready to take on the world, if needed. When you are inspired, you feel energized, awake, sharp, vibrant.

Inspiration is a spiritual phenomenon.

Inspiration awakens us to new possibilities by allowing us to transcend our ordinary experiences and limitations. Inspiration propels a person from apathy to possibility, and transforms the way we perceive our own capabilities.

Inspiration is effortless.

Unlike motivation, where you are compelled by external factors to take action, inspiration is a driving force that comes from the inside. We all need a little inspiration and uplifting spirit, now more than ever.

Today, I would like to uplift your spirit and offer you a gift.

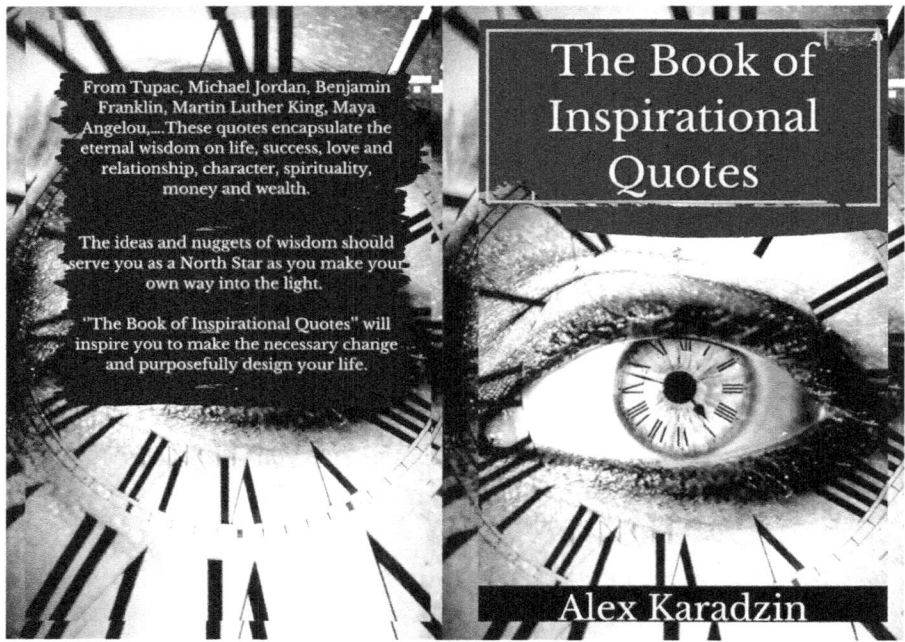

The Book of Inspirational Quotes

From Tupac, Michael Jordan, Benjamin Franklin, Martin Luther King, Maya Angelou,....These quotes encapsulate the eternal wisdom on life, success, love and relationship, character, spirituality, money and wealth.

The ideas and nuggets of wisdom should serve you as a North Star as you make your own way into the light. ''The Book of Inspirational Quotes'' will inspire you to make the necessary change and purposefully design your life.

In this book, you will find quotes, thoughts and ideas from the brightest minds in our history.

The *Inspirational Book of Quotes* consists of inspirational and transformational quotes on life, success, love and relationship, character, spirituality, money and wealth.

Claim your free copy by visiting:

https://connectionrockstar.com/the-book-of-inspirational-quotes/

About the Author

From one reader to another – I'd like to welcome you to the most exclusive arbitrary 'Cover to Cover Book Club!' I appreciate you for taking a few moments to get to know me.

My name is Alex Karadzin. A proud Serbian, born in beautiful Bosnia in a great country once known as Yugoslavia.

I am a multimedia artist, a lifelong student, and a modern-day teacher.

Ever since I was a child, I was encouraged by my family to explore as far as the outer limits of my mind go. My curious attitude towards life and my wondrous spirit led me to many unusual places.

One of them being the nightlife industry.

For about two years, I was a nightlife photographer living the rock and roll lifestyle to the fullest. Through my nightlife job and this social environment, I have learned so much about human psychology and social dynamics, but most of all I learned so much about myself.

Aside from photography, I am an amateur actor and writer. As of recently, I have started playing and practicing the guitar.

My other interests and passion include philosophy, spirituality, history, fitness, and mixed martial arts. I have various hobbies that mostly include some aspect of self-development rituals in them.

I am an avid content consumer and a voracious reader. Life-long learning is just deeply ingrained into the very essence of my being.

Knowing "Who I am" is my Northstar for what I do professionally.

I work as a Learning and Transformational Designer. My job is to create a framework for the learning experience that takes place in the physical or digital world.

Physically in the form of: Seminars and training, various types of conferences, and live events.

In an online format, I do most of my work as an online content and course creator, mostly in the domain of personal development.

I have been part of the industry for the last 6 years, working in one of the biggest companies in the world, Mindvalley.

In 2018, I've decided to follow my heart and soul and leave Malaysia to work on my personal projects and ventures. One of them was the Connection Rockstar Platform with the idea of bringing brilliant people together to learn and eventually, to teach others. The content on the platform was primarily about social dynamics, human psychology, and behavior. Over time, I have experimented with different content formats and different content consumer experience.

As of 2021, I am still on a never-ending quest of challenging the status quo as I expand the limits of my perception, searching for answers and wisdom that comes with those answers.

As I go along my journey, I want to share that wisdom, serve, and encourage others to be rockstars and live their life to the fullest. I believe in the idea that everybody can live a meaningful life on their terms. Life is about freedom, experiences, people, and ultimately...contribution.

In the words of great Neal Donald Walch:

"Your life is not about you. Your life is about everyone else whose life you touch and the way in which you do so."

Also by Alex Karadzin

If you are interested in developing your charisma and improving your social skills, I recommend checking out my work on the subject.

Relationships are the core of your success. Success is defined by you, of course. However, regardless of how you define it — to achieve that success, you'll need other people. The opportunities for success are all around you and more often than not — those opportunities unveil themselves through the people you meet along your journey.

Life is so much easier when you have relationships that can elevate you and your current circumstances. I would dare to say that pretty much everything I've achieved is directly correlated with my ability to create, maintain, and grow my relationships.

The ability to create and develop deep and meaningful social connections, nurture and grow relationships, is a measure of true success.

Charisma Rockstar: The Unique Blueprint For Owning Your Charisma

For years, we've been told that Charisma is an elusive and exclusive gift reserved for the chosen few. The superpower to inspire devotion in others with your presence, words, and action is the only one you'll ever need.

Charisma Rockstar offers you everything you need to know to develop the charismatic mindset and attitude. With this blueprint, charming and winning people over will become your second nature. Making a memorable impression will become a part of your personality, your charisma DNA.

Here is what you'll learn:

· How to develop a charismatic attitude

· The crucial charisma ingredient for any social interaction

· The easiest way to start a conversation

· How to find and pull the emotional trigger

· How to calibrate, backtrack and save the conversation

· How to deal with haters and critics

· Controversial and unorthodox principles of networking

· ''Outside of the box'' approach of highly charismatic individuals

And much, much more...

Here is how Charisma Rockstar is structured:

The first part is an introduction to the concept of charisma. We are going to cover some of the biggest misconceptions about charisma, as well as debunk the myth about charismatic people.

The second part of the book is all about building a solid foundation. The charisma foundation is crucial before you even have the opportunity to interact with people in any social environment. In here, you will learn the mindset you should develop so that you can shine when it matters the most to you.

Last, but not the least is all about creating magic. When you have that foundation ready and stable, creating a memorable impression will become your second nature. You'll stand out from the crowd and shine when it matters to you. This is exactly what the third and final part of the book is about. Creating the Charisma Effect on anyone, anywhere.

Bonus Content
Secret Charisma Weapon of Dwayne 'The Rock' Johnson
Chris Hemsworth Charisma Mindset & Attitude
[Case Study] Jonah Hill Fat Shaming

Your Social Skills Guidebook: How to Talk to Anyone; Network with Confidence and Make Social Connections
'Success is a journey, not a destination''

We have heard this expression before but what does it mean?

Regardless of your definition of success, one thing is undeniable. Your success, just like your life – isn't about you. Your life is about everyone else whose life you touch and the manner in which you do so.

The ability to create and develop deep and meaningful social connections, nurture and grow relationships, is the only measure of true success.

The greatest luxury in life is a social luxury. With this guide, you will increase your social value and learn how to acquire that social luxury.

You will discover how to:

· Use small talk as a gateway to a deep social connection

· Be the life of any party

· Tell memorable stories and keep your audience engaged

· Listen with intention and earn people's trust

· Make a memorable first impression and network like a boss

· Start and lead a conversation and make a lasting social connection

· Tap into your inner charisma and how to express your unique charismatic

94

self

How the roadmap looks like:

Your Social Skills Guidebook has three parts.

Social Skills Fundamentals is the first part.

When it comes to social skills, there are a few fundamental things we can do to make social connections: Firstly, the ability to relate with others and earn their trust. To do so, we need to know how to make small talk work for us and how to listen with intention. In this part, we will also explore the power of storytelling and keeping people engaged while telling the story.

Networking is the second part of this book.

Here, the focus is primarily on the ongoing conversation in the larger social context that is networking. You will learn how to strike up the conversation and how to keep it going. We will cover the topic of the first impression from a different angle. I will share with you my personal techniques for remembering names and effectively using it to create deeper social connections.

Charisma is the last part of this book.

There are a lot of misconceptions and a veil of mystery surrounding the subject of charisma. As you will discover, charisma is nothing more than the result of the right attitude, exceptional communication and interpersonal skills. In this part, we will focus on the more advanced concepts of social skills such as: the philosophy of self-amusement, dealing with haters and verbal bullies, recognizing and pulling someone's emotional trigger, and additional methods for expanding your awareness.

[Kobe Bryant] Success Mindset: 5 Pillars of The Mamba Mindset

On January 26, 2020, the world stood still as the news emerged that Kobe Bryant, his daughter Gianna and seven others lost their lives in a helicopter accident. In the year of pandemic, fearmongering and unprecedented division between humanity, the tragic loss of one of the greatest basketball players can sadly be neglected.

Kobe Bryant was one of the greatest players that ever graced the basketball court. He was famous for his relentless drive to win and succeed. He was famous for his mindset – The Mamba Mentality.

This book is a short guide designed as a learning experience for the reader. Kobe was an incredible teacher as he taught me how to play the game of life and win.

Through the short powerful stories and examples from Kobe's life, we will explore the Mamba Mindset through the following 5 pillars:

Life Vission
·Curiosity
·Work Ethic
·The Fundamentals
·Mentors

This guidebook is not for you:

1. If you expect to find facts and statistics.

2. Dry facts and numbers about Kobe's life and career are available elsewhere.

This guidebook is for you if:

1. You are a basketball and Kobe Bryant fan.
2. You are curious to know about the legendary Mamba Mentality and maybe apply concepts as you develop your success mindset.

'' We all have self-doubt. You don't deny it, but you also don't capitulate to it. You embrace it.'' – Kobe Bryant

Exclusive from the "Success Leaves Clues" series.

Dwayne 'The Rock' Johnson: Success Mindset, Habits, and Life Lessons

Dwayne 'The Rock' Johnson, a former professional wrestler, the most bankable movie star in the world, and a wildly successful entrepreneur – *The Rock shows us that dreams do come true.*

His success story serves as an inspiration but more importantly, The Rock shows us how to be authentic in this noisy world.

In this success guide, we will take a deeper look at the life of Dwayne 'The Rock' Johnson and deconstruct his powerful success models.

This guidebook is designed as a learning experience for the reader. In it, we'll cover the following aspects of The Rock's unique personality and success:

The Origin Story
· Introspection Mindset & Attitude
· Vulnerability
· Self-Amusement
· Conviction & Charisma

Additionally, there is a breakdown of each chapter and a concrete 'How To' aspect you can model and replicate in your everyday life.

This guidebook is not for you if:
You expect to find facts and a list of accomplishments. Dry facts about The Rock's life and career are available elsewhere.

This guidebook is for you if:
1. You are a true fan of Dwayne 'The Rock' Johnson.
2. You are into personal development and you want to see a detailed breakdown

of The Rock's success mindset, habits, and life lessons.

Exclusive from the "Success Leaves Clues" series.

Made in the USA
Coppell, TX
16 December 2021

68920893R00059